CURIOUS
DEVON

CURIOUS
DEVON

DERRICK WARREN

First published in the United Kingdom in 2008

Reprinted in 2008 by The History Press
The Mill, Brimscombe Port, Stroud,
Gloucestershire, GL5 2QG
www.thehistorypress.co.uk

Reprinted 2011, 2012, 2013

British Library Cataloguing in Publication Data
A catalogue record for this book is available from the British Library.

ISBN 978-0-7509-4886-9

To the late 'Chips' Barber for his inspirational love and knowledge of Devonshire, and to my daughter, Louise, for her persistent encouragement.

Typeset in 11/13.5 Janson
Typesetting and origination by
The History Press.
Printed and bound in England.

CONTENTS

AUTHOR'S NOTE

Devonshire is the second largest county in England and certainly has its fair share of the curious and odd, both old and new. From the narrowest street in the world to the largest square and smallest village in the country; from peculiar railways to unusual castles; from telling the time to pointing the way; from crossing rivers to looking to the stars, to say nothing of the devil and even stranger creatures!

However, this is neither a guide nor a history of the county, although inevitably history has its place, for Devon holds a great deal of the country's history, with many characters of note, but these have been excluded except where they are connected with an object or place. Some of the subjects are well known but have a slant to the story, such as Kent's Cavern in Torquay; as for Clovelly, how could it possibly not be included?

Included here is a very personal and idiosyncratic collection of places, facts and stories gleaned while I was working for the Ordnance Survey as a (very inquisitive) surveyor, living in Devon and hugely enjoying this glorious county. I knew of every subject, with few exceptions, before starting this book, although I did not know everything there was to know about them; so compiling this book has been a fascinating exercise as I revisited all the places, some of which I had not seen for many years, and to find out more about them, correcting a few misconceptions and unearthing some surprises along the way.

I have largely passed over Devon's magnificent churches, for they have been more than covered by others. Churchyards are another matter, for they hold a mine of information and little gems of local history! Where a town or village is not included, it does not mean that it holds nothing of interest, just that I did not know of it; neither, for the same reason, have I tried to balance the entries across the county. For locals, I hope that I have reminded them of what they have, while showing visitors something of Devonshire's secrets.

The entries are in alphabetical order by location, with the prefix number corresponding to those on the location map on page viii. Most can be seen or visited from a public road or path (or are open on payment of a fee), and the map references should enable them to be found easily (Ordnance Survey Landranger Series, sheets 190, 191, 192, 193, 201 and 202). However, even though a map reference is given, it does not necessarily mean that there is public access or that they are on private property – in these instances I have tried to make that clear in the text; in one case I have deliberately omitted the map reference.

Except where individually acknowledged, all the photographs and illustrations are from my own collection.

Derrick Warren
Taunton, 2007

ACKNOWLEDGEMENTS

I should like to thank all those who so generously shared their research and knowledge with me, those who allowed me to photograph and wander over their property, and to all the kind people who helped in the compilation of this book in so many ways. Without them my task would have been infinitely more arduous and would not have afforded me the pleasure of sharing their interests and enthusiasm. In particular, I must thank Sally Barber for permission to use extracts from my booklet *East Devon Curiosities*, which was published by her late husband's Obelisk Press.

A thank you also to the following:

Ron Ackland, Shebbear; Lady Arran, Filleigh; Martin Bodman, Cullompton; H. Boyer, Combe Martin; David Bromwich, Somerset Local Studies Library; James Broughton, Ashburton Museum; Ruth Carvosso, Tawstock; Frankie Cawthorne, Dartmouth Museum; Bob Chambers, Minehead; Chris Chapman, Three Hares Project, Throwleigh; John Christie, Bideford; James Coulter, Tawstock; A.O. Cook, Churchdon; William Davies, Yelverton; Simon Dell, Devon & Cornwall Police, Exeter; Devon Record Office, Exeter; Beryl Docker, Ugborough History Group; Jackie Edwards, Braunton & District Museum; Sue Gehan, Barnstaple Local History Library; the late Mary Glanvill, Chard; Dr Peter Glanvill, Chard; John Hadfield, Bideford; Mrs M. Harper, Mamhead; Trevor Hitchcock, Honiton Museum; David Hunt, Wokingham; Mike Jones, Taunton; Valerie Lister, Bicton; Revd Sandra Lloydlangham, Exmouth; Mrs M. Loftus, Halberton; Bob Lush, Tiverton Museum; Andy Mantus, Watcombe; Allan Mills, Leicester; G.S.C. Millstrom, Woolhanger; Brian Murless, Taunton; Netson Owen, Sidbury; Graham Rowland, Ottery St Mary; John Scott, Beer; John Shields, North Tawton; Dr Peter Stanier, Shaftsbury; J. Turner, Lawrence Castle; Adam Warren, Southampton; Louise Warren, London; D. Webster, Manaton; West Country Studies Library, Exeter; Gerald White, Sidmouth; Anthony Mildmay-White, Flete; Pat Winslow, Sidbury; Keneth Woodley, Newton Poppleford; Richard Willey, Taunton; Simon Wills, Babbacombe.

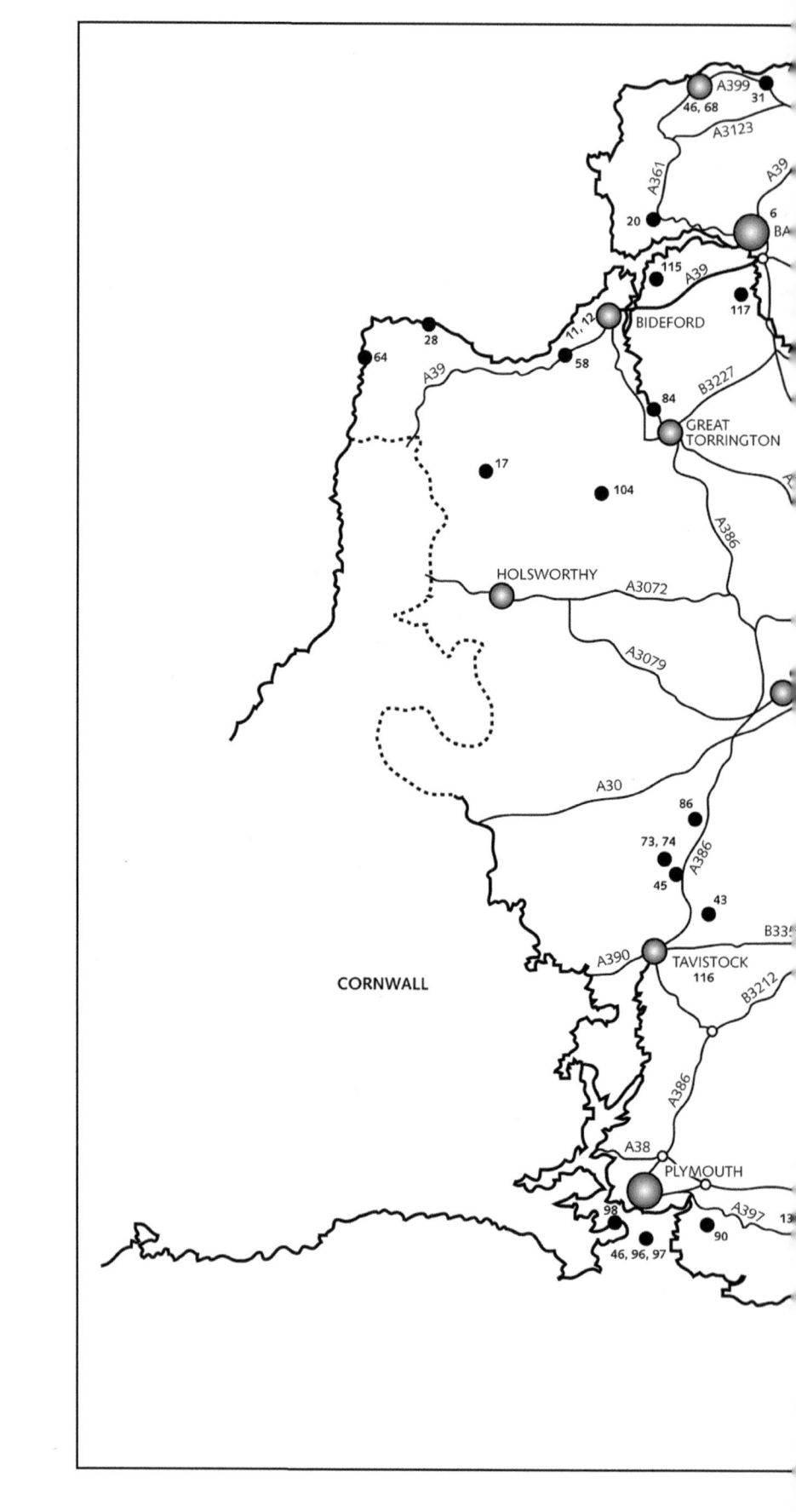

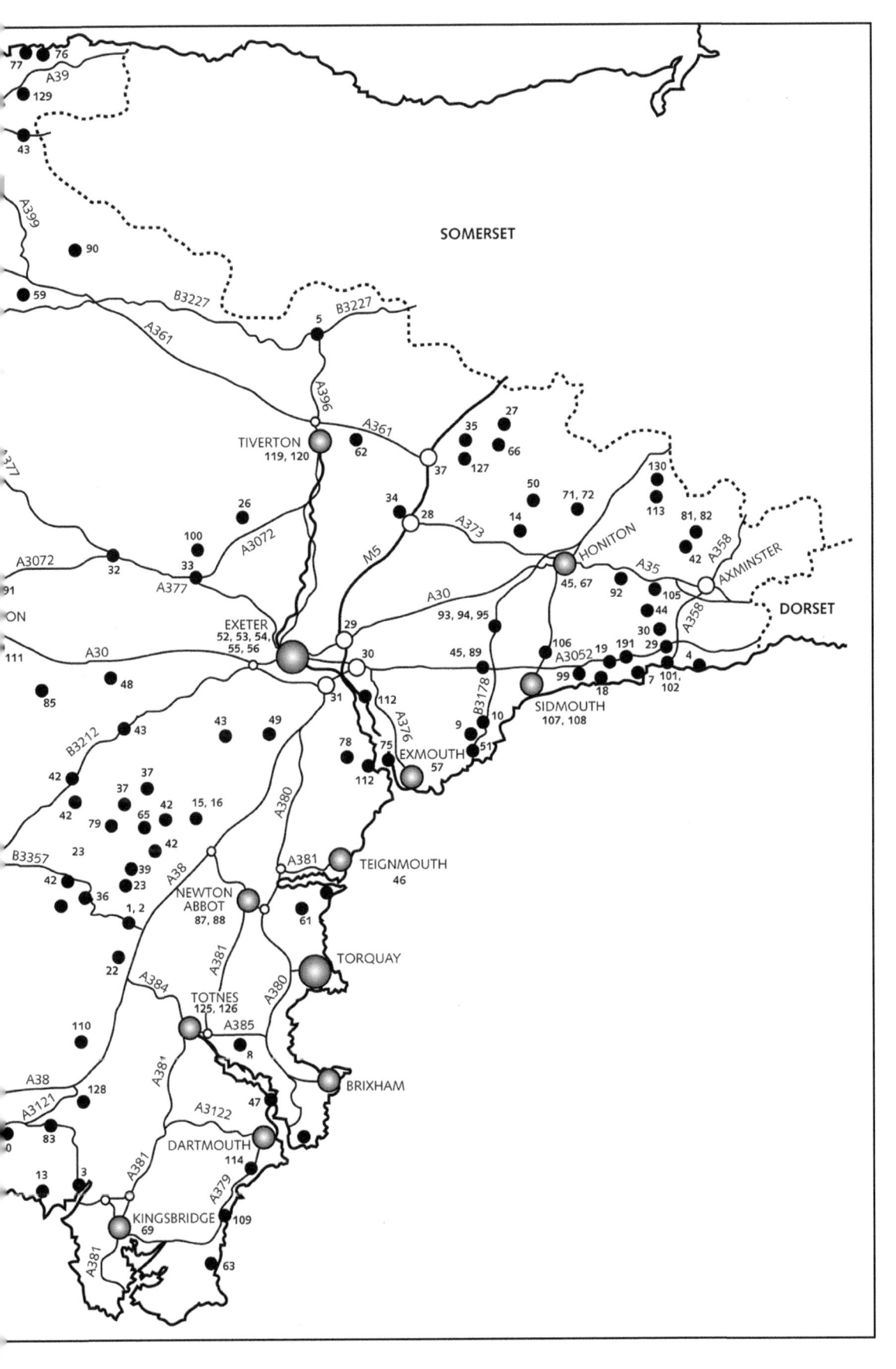

Saddle Horse Bridge over the River Bovey.

A–Z OF THE
CURIOSITIES OF DEVON

1

Map Ref
SX755699

ASHBURTON

The Gaming House

A feature of many houses in Totnes, Kingsbridge and Ashburton are their slate-hung frontages. The dividing walls, with their fireplaces, are of stone construction but the front and back of the buildings have boarded timber framing on which are hung slates, quarried locally.

Many of the slates on the former gaming house at 10 North Street, Ashburton, have been cut to represent the pips of the four suits, which have been grouped together to form patterns of the various suits – hearts, diamonds, clubs and spades. Each individual pip has been cut from two or three slates, some being scalloped along the bottom edge. They are hung from the top by a single nail and cemented out at an angle.

Sadly, nothing is recorded about the gaming house, but it is clear that the cut slates were a form of advertisement for what went on within.

Dating the house is also difficult; the style of the sash windows was only introduced into London in about 1690; so allowing for the lapse in time for new ideas to reach Devon, the house probably dates from about 1700, around the time when gambling with cards was a very popular pastime; the owner must have had means, for the framing is of oak. The house is a little bit of history that, tantalisingly, has no history! The decorative features were restored in 1989 with help from the Dartmoor National Park and English Heritage; it has now, after many different uses, become a small supermarket.

Frontage of the
Gaming House.

ASHBURTON

The Wild West

Devonshire seems an improbable place to find an important collection of Native American artefacts. It all started in about 1990, when Paul Endecott from Oklahoma, USA, visited Ashburton to see where his forebears lived. As a personal thank you to Ashburton Museum, on returning to the USA he, with the help of the Paramount Chief of the Cherokees and Patrick Pattersen, the curator of the Native American Museum, bought a representative collection of artefacts of the tribes of the Northern Plains over several years, all of which are over 150 years old and all with provenances to the correct tribe and the original owners.

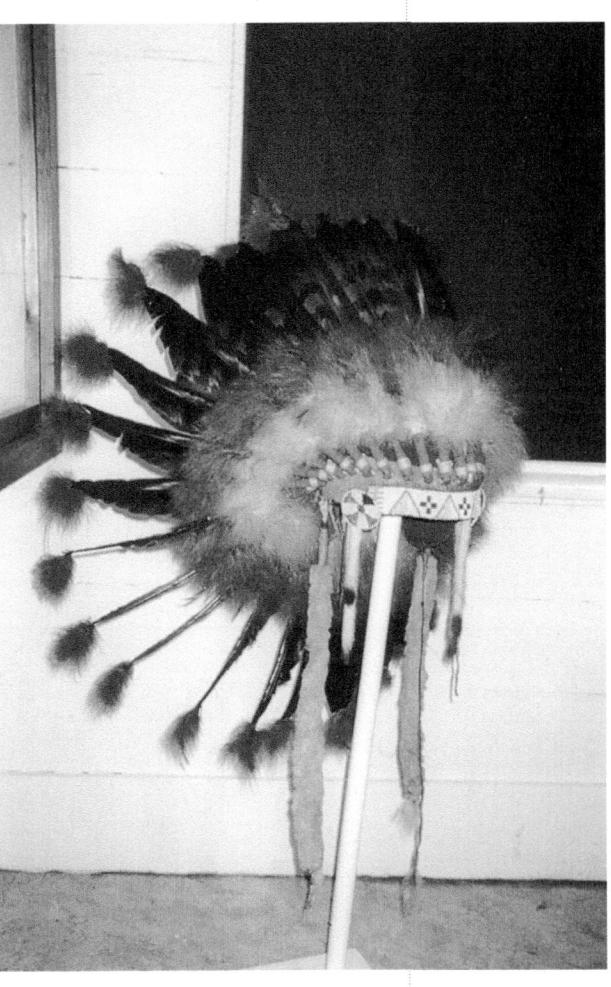

Sioux war bonnet.

This collection now occupies the top floor of the Ashburton Museum. Two of the most interesting items are a Sioux war bonnet, each eagle feather being a record of tribal valour as well as individual deeds by the wearer, and the beautiful doe-skin dress of a Cheyenne squaw. The collection also features toy sleds of the Seneca, one containing a baby doll; a Navajo squaw travelling rug; bow and arrows and a tomahawk of the Cherokees; a Kaw tomahawk; an Armaho 'Coup stick' (a young warrior had to stalk an enemy, touch him on the shoulder with the Coup stick and then try and escape); a medicine man's bag with contents and from a much earlier era, flint tools and arrowheads. This is a superb collection and is unique in Britain. It is open to the public from spring until autumn.

3

Map Ref
SX672467–
SX692472

AVETON GIFFORD

Tidal Road

Many roads situated near rivers having creeks or inlets had short stretches which at high tide were covered by water; few of them were of any great length, and where this did occur, the advent of the motor vehicle has led to their elevation. (The road between Axmouth and Axmouth harbour is a good example of this.)

At Aveton Gifford, however, the road to Bigbury and St Ann's Chapel runs alongside the tidal estuary of the River Avon for three quarters of a mile; with mud flats, flocks of seabirds and wildfowl on one side and low cliffs and hanging woods on the other, before the road climbs steeply up to Bigbury. Even at medium tide, most of the road is underwater, with posts on either side of the road at the deeper stretches, where it dips down or crosses a creek. Locals, should they risk it, can save nearly 5 miles by taking this road to Bigbury, but many have miscalculated the depth, especially at night, and only recently (December 2006), an elderly couple had to be rescued after their car left the road and was completely submerged half an hour later! Yet, on a nice day in the spring or summer, it can be a delightful drive or walk.

Tidal Road at low tide, looking north.

AXMOUTH

The Landslip

4

Map Ref
SY285295

The geology between Axmouth harbour and Lyme Regis has always made the cliffs unstable and liable to slipping, forming wide undercliffs. The cataclysm which occurred in 1839, however, was on an entirely different scale.

During the early hours of 25 December, a half-mile long fissure appeared in the fields of Dowlands Farm, above Bindon Cliffs. Farm workers and their families were awoken at about 4 a.m. by the walls of their cottages groaning and cracking open; all escaped safely but had to scramble in the darkness up a 20ft cliff where the path to the farm had been. During the following two days the fissure widened to over 300ft and in some places, was over 150ft deep. Some of the southernmost fields and hedges, although sinking some 80ft, remained level, with this area becoming known as 'the island', and the crops with which it had been planted being harvested the following summer!

On 26 December, a reef, about half a mile long and 40ft high, was pushed up from the seabed about 200 yards offshore, remaining for several years until being worn away by the sea. By the evening of the 26th, all major movement had ceased and the area has remained much the same ever since except, that is, for the luxuriant vegetation – tree, scrub, bramble and creeper – which has grown up and obscured much of it.

The landslip before the trees grew up, *c.* 1905.

The undercliffs are now designated a Site of Scientific Importance (SSI) and are managed by English Nature. The 'island' was long kept clear by rabbits, but since their numbers were depleted by myxomatosis, it is now cut periodically to preserve the rare flora growing there. The remaining area is now virtually impenetrable and because of hidden fissures and cliffs, is extremely dangerous. There is, however, a public footpath running from the top of Bindon Cliff to Lyme Regis; about 7 miles of fairly rough walking in a fascinating wilderness.

5

**Map Ref
SS957222**

BAMPTON

An Odd Memorial

Set into the west wall of the tower of the church of St Michael and All Angels is an inscribed stone, with an extremely odd view of a tragic event. It reads:

> In Memory of the Clerk's son
> Bless my iiiii [eyes]
> Here he lies
> In a sad pickle
> Killed by icicle
> In the Year 1776

As this is a replacement stone for the original, which had become too worn to be read, the people of Bampton must have appreciated the somewhat macabre humour!

BARNSTAPLE

The Tome Stone

6
Map Ref
SS557330

During the sixteenth and seventeenth centuries, Barnstaple was an important and thriving port trading extensively with Europe, Ireland and North America, only declining in importance during the eighteenth century with the silting-up of the River Taw.

The beautiful, colonnaded Merchant's Walk or Exchange stood alongside a slipway of the Great Quay, opposite the town's old Watergate. It was cut off from the quay when the slipway was filled in to allow the railway into the town in 1874.

The merchant's business was concluded on the quayside over the Tome Stone, a circular, flat stone set on a pedestal, which served as a 'counter' on which, during a transaction, the money changing hands would be placed, thus making the bargain legally binding. This was similar in size and purpose to the cast-iron nail outside Bristol's Market House, where the expression 'paid on the nail' arose. The present Tome Stone dates from about 1633 and around its edge are inscribed the names of three of the town's worthies: John Delbridge (merchant and three-times mayor); Nicholas Delbridge (alderman) and Richard Ferris (former mayor).

With the erection of a statue of Queen Anne in the late seventeenth century, the name Merchant's Walk was changed to Queen Anne's

Queen Anne's Walk and the site of the Tome Stone.

The Tome Stone,
c. 1930. *(Knights)*

Walk. The Tome Stone was transferred to its present position directly under the statue in 1900 and is protected with iron railings; although not protected enough, it seems, for in 2006 it was knocked off its pedestal and is (at the time of writing) in the museum awaiting repair.

7

Map Ref
SY214893

BEER

Smuggling and Beer Caves

During the late eighteenth and early nineteenth centuries, smuggling was rife along the south coast of England and nowhere more so than in East Devon. The isolated, narrow valleys of Branscombe, Littlecombe, Weston and Salcombe, leading down to shelving shingle beaches, were ideal for this trade, with the haven of Beer and its fishing fleet as its headquarters. The lengths to which the preventive service eventually went to try to control this coast can be seen in the line of coastguard cottages at Branscombe (now a single house) and the ruins of similar ones at Weston.

Smugglers are often depicted in a romantic light but in reality, most came into the trade because of poverty and the harsh conditions under which many farm labourers and fishermen lived, and they did so to supplement their meagre earnings. They had to fight a continuous duel with the preventive men and the riding officers, and only became violent to evade capture and the forfeiture of their boats.

Jack (John) Rattenbury, however, was not of this violent mould and lived to become known as 'The Rob Roy of the West'. He was born in Beer on 18 October 1778. He first went to sea at the age of fourteen, and at sixteen he was press-ganged into the Navy. He escaped and became, not very successfully, a privateer until he was twenty-five. On 17 April 1801, he married a local girl and had to think of a steady living, so for thirty years he became a smuggler, enjoying the money and the thrill of the 'game', and because he was never violent, Jack was never actively pursued by the law – only by the Navy as a deserter!

JOHN RATTENBURY.
of Beer, Devonshire
"THE ROB ROY of the WEST"

A sketch of Jack Rattenbury: 'the Rob Roy of the West'. (*Devonshire Characters and Strange Events,* S. Baring-Gould)

At the age of fifty-eight, finding himself on hard times, Jack was given a pension of a shilling a week by John, Baron Rolle, for his work in connection with building seawalls at Sidmouth and Exmouth. (For a few years he had been a contractor for hydraulic lime.) By 1837, his exploits had become widely known throughout the West Country and in that year he published his autobiography *Memoirs of a Smuggler*, although from the style of the prose, it was almost certainly 'ghosted' by someone else. Jack died on 28 April 1844 and is buried in an unmarked grave in the churchyard of St Gregory's, Seaton.

*   *   *

Nowhere are Jack's romantic exploits and those of other smugglers brought to light more evocatively than in Beer Caves, the vast underground quarries, worked for stone since Roman times and from which a great deal was used in the building of Exeter Cathedral and other local churches and houses. The two types of stone hewn were ideal for building, for although easy to carve, they soon became hard on exposure to the air. The caves were used for religious meetings by

A section of
the caves.
(John Scott)

the Dissenters, and tradition has it that Jack Rattenbury and his fellow
smugglers used the caves for storing their illicit brandy, tobacco, etc.
This has recently been confirmed by the discovery of the remains of
brandy barrels in a hitherto unexplored area of the caves.

The caves are open to the public during the summer months and
occasional days during the winter, and have become a well-known
visitor attraction.

Visitors are not the only guests at the caves, for they are also a
nationally important nesting site for bats during the winter, and
provision has been made for them to get in and out of the caves.
Those coming to the caves to hibernate during September and
October include Bechstein's bat, the greater and lesser horseshoe bat,
Natterer's bat, Daubenton's bat, the brown long-eared bat, whiskered
bat and Brandt's bat.

When Judith Maria Waldron of Bovey House married John,
Second Baron Rolle in 1778, she concerned herself with the welfare
of those who lived on her husband's estates. Accustomed as she would
have been to the pure water from the well at Bovey House (see p. 23),
when she visited Beer in 1780, she was distressed to find that the main
source of drinking water in the village was from the stream which
flowed down the main street, which was used as a convenient way of
disposing household waste, fish heads, etc. Lady Rolle had two stone
conduits built across the stream (SY229893), each with a spout from

which gushed a constant flow of pure water piped from a spring at the top of the village. In the late nineteenth century, a cast-iron conduit was sited further down the street.

One of Lady Waldron's conduits.

Lord Rolle, no doubt, also appreciated pure water to add to his brandy – possibly provided by Jack Rattenbury, for it is known that he had much sympathy for him as evidenced by the pension.

BERRY POMEROY

Parliament Cottage

8

Map Ref
SX836596

With no Protestant successor to the throne, William, Duke of Orange, was invited by the British Parliament to come to England and accept the crown.

On a foggy November day in 1688, he landed at Brixham to be greeted by the gentlemen of Devon. With his followers he marched north through the narrow Devon lanes with drums beating and trumpets blowing until he neared the hamlet of Longcombe, where he halted at a cottage and held his first parliament on British soil. He then marched on to Berry Pomeroy where he was received by Sir Edward Seymour at Berry Pomeroy Castle while, it is said, his followers feasted on a field of turnips!

Parliament House.

In the garden of the cottage now stands a stone, 4ft high and 1ft 3in wide, on which are the words 'William, Prince of Orange, is said to have held the first Parliament here in November 1688'. Of far greater interest is the cottage, for it still stands on the left of the narrow road which leads to Longcombe, in the parish of Berry Pomeroy. It was, however, far from being a cottage; more the home of a well-to-do yeoman or a member of the local gentry, although compared to the great houses William was used to, it would have seemed humble indeed.

Built from cob under a thatched roof, it has a wing abutting on to the road, three projecting gables to the south and three tall, tapering stone chimneys. It is everything a typical Devon cottage should be, and should one feel inclined to spend the night in 'Parliament House', as it is now called, one can, for it now offers bed and breakfast. Incidentally, on the 1:50,000 OS map the cottage is simply called 'Parliament'.

BICTON

Brick Cross

The crossroads where the road to Otterton leaves the B3178 has taken its name from the tall, brick column surmounted by a stone cross which once acted as a direction post, with the place names inscribed upon inset stone squares. Curiously, the place names face the direction from which the traveller has come; Budley [*sic*], Littleham and Exmouth face south, Woodbury, Topsham and Exeter face west, Bicton, Ottery and Honiton face north and Otterton, Sidmouth and Colliton [*sic*] face east!

It was erected in 1743 by Lady Rolle of Bicton House, and is also known as the Scripture Stone due to the quotations taken from the Bible which are inscribed near the top of its four sides:

> Make me go in the path of Thy
> Commandments for therein is my
> desire
> Oh, that our ways were made so
> direct that we might keep Thy
> Statutes
> Oh, hold Thou up our going in Thy
> path that our feet shall slip not
> Her way is the way of pleasantness
> and all her paths are peace

Brick Cross with obelisk of Bicton gardens.

A sort of eighteenth-century moral Highway Code, providing good texts for sermons to be thought out while walking through the countryside!

10

Map Ref
SY073858

BICTON

Bicton Gardens

Thinking of gardens in a West Country context, thoughts invariably go to Cornwall and its subtropical and tropical gardens; many, however, would be hard put to think of any in Devon – with one exception; those at Bicton, near Budleigh Salterton. This garden has so much to offer; a magnificent domed glass Palm House, the second largest in Britain and twenty years older than the one at Kew; as well as the Pinetum, the lake, the American and Japanese gardens, and trains for children (and adults!).

But what make Bicton so special, and curious, is the incomparable Italianate Garden – the only one in the West Country and probably the finest in Britain. Constructed by Henry, the first Baron Rolle, in about 1735 to the design of Andre Le Notre (the man who laid out the sumptuous garden at the Palace of Versailles, near Paris). Italianate Gardens differ entirely from the 'garden landscapes' that were being laid out by Capability Brown and others during the same period, and although both styles rely on vistas, one is formal and the other artificially natural.

At Bicton the garden is best seen from the Orangery, built much later in about 1812, with the long axis of the garden sweeping down over flowerbeds, statuary, ponds and fountains to the formal lake and fountain, then over the 'canal' at the bottom and up through a sunken avenue of trees to the focal point in the far distance, an obelisk. This garden is nowhere near Lord Rolle's house but Le Notre saw the geography of the site and designed the garden to fit it – to glorious effect.

Bicton's Italianate gardens, with the canal in the foreground.

BIDEFORD

The Little Newsboy

11
Map Ref
SS451267

High on top of the gable of a butcher's shop in Mill Street stands the statue of a little newsboy selling papers, for this building was once the offices of the local newspaper, the *Western Express* (1876–1919). He is affectionately known as the Ragged Little Newsboy, for the bottom of his trousers are in tatters, one knee sticks out through a hole and he has bare feet; a regular little urchin were it not for his rather sweet face. He was also once known as the Dirty Little Newsboy, not for any lack of cleanliness, but because of the salacious nature of the articles which regularly appeared in the *Western Express*.

Sadly, during the autumn of 2006, the statue disappeared. The premises are due for redevelopment, but as the whole of Mill Street is scheduled, the frontage, together with the Little Newsboy, should be retained. It is said that he fell off (backwards) and the town awaits his return.

The Little
Newsboy.
(John Hadfield)

12
Map Ref
SS456244

BIDEFORD

The Long Bridge

The Long Bridge of Bideford is well named for it measures 677ft long and has twenty-four arches. It is these that make the bridge so unusual for each arch has a different width span.

The name Bideford stems from Beuda's Ford, which was the first place up the River Torridge (which means rough river) where it could be forded. By the end of the thirteenth century, trade made a bridge essential. The parish priest at Bideford, Richard Gurney, was the driving force behind its building, financially assisted by the leading local family, the Grenville's, and Peter Quivel, Bishop of Exeter, who granted a licence for 'indulgancies' to be sold at chapels at each end of the bridge to help finance it and for its maintenance. It was an oak timber bridge, just wide enough for packhorses and pedestrians and was completed in about 1290. It was a major medieval engineering feat, although it had to be built in stages as money became available. Because of this, several groups of carpenters and craftsmen were involved at different times, resulting in the different widths of the arch spans!

After 170 years, the bridge became in danger of collapsing. A completely new bridge was financially impractical, so the timber supports were encased by masonry, the bridge widened and cut-waters built onto bedrock to help support it and to give 'refuges' for pedestrians to avoid the pack trains. To make it suitable for wheeled traffic, it was widened in 1792–1810, again in 1865 and 1925, but was saved further remedial work by the construction of the graceful Torridge Bridge, just short of a mile downstream, in 1987.

The Long Bridge. *(Author's Collection)*

BIGBURY

An Eagle Owl

13
Map Ref
SX668467

A keen ornithologist will tell you that the Eagle Owl is a rare sighting in this country, but one can be seen on any day in Bigbury!

In about 1510, Bishop Oldham of Exeter gave St Andrew's, the parish church at Ashburton, a new pulpit and lectern; the lectern was somewhat unusual, for instead of the usual eagle this was an owl; the bishop's badge or crest.

In 1777, St Lawrence's Church at Bigbury was in need both of a new pulpit and lectern. Ashburton saw the chance of disposing of their unwanted gifts and sold both to Bigbury for £11. The parishioners at Bigbury must have bought a 'pig in a poke', for they were not at all pleased with the owl lectern; after all, the eagle was invariably depicted as being the most suitable creature to hold the Bible, being able to fly nearest to God.

The priest also had a reason for not liking it, claiming that he did not like the way the owl looked at him! So the unfortunate owl was sent to a craftsman at Plymouth for a new head; fortunately it was, again unusually, made of wood, so the head was sawn off and the head of an eagle substituted. Today, the very obvious owl's body, feathers, wings and huge clawed feet has the head and beak of an eagle – a very long and wicked beak at that!

Golden eagle, looking purposefully away from pulpit and preacher!

BLACKBOROUGH

14

Map Ref
ST099083–
ST105064

Whetstone Mines

Just under the steep escarpment which extends from Blackborough towards Broadhembury is a track way. On the higher, east side of this can still be seen the depressions which mark the dozens of collapsed adits, or tunnels, which were driven into the hillside to extract the special sandstone suitable for use as whetstones. In the days when crops were either cut by a scythe or a sickle, the shaped whetstone was used to sharpen the blades and was an important and valuable item of farm equipment. The mines were worked for almost 200 years, mainly by miners from Cornwall who took the whetstones to the main market for this trade at Exeter. The mines did not close until the end of the nineteenth century, when the more efficient carborundum stones became commonplace.

Shaping a
whetstone,
c. 1851. *(Devon
Record Office)*

Upon the promontory of this escarpment, at the end of the present gliding club's runway, is an area of broken ground with

Mode of trimming Whet-stones for scythes on the Whet-stone Hills, Punchey Down, and one of the entrances into the side of the hill. This passage entered 300 yards horizontally.   Sketched Sept.ʳ 12, 1854.

circular depressions. These, however, have nothing to do with the whetstone mines but are the remains of bell-pits, where from Roman to medieval times, bog iron was mined to support the local iron-smelting trade.

The collapsed adits today.

BOVEY TRACEY

John Cann's Lane

15
Map Ref
SX816798

In 1644 the Parliamentary forces under Cromwell took their Royalist opponents by surprise on Bovey Heath and defeated them; no wonder, for their officers were carousing in a hostelry in Bovey Tracey. When the Roundheads arrived outside the inn, the officers threw their money out of the windows into the road and while this was being scrabbled for by the soldiery (or 'distracted' as a contemporary account puts it) they made their escape. One, John Cann, had the presence of mind to take the Royalists' treasure chest with him, but being heavy, when he reached the top of the hill outside Bovey, he buried it in the dark among some large rocks in a wood beside the lane. Although he returned to search for the chest, it was never found, for the wood is as full of large rocks as it is of trees. It is said that John

Cann's ghost still searches the wood for his buried treasure.) The story of John Cann is still alive locally, with the name John Cann's Lane shown on the large scale Ordnance maps, and although the lane is now only a rough track through the woods, it remains a right of way.

Up steep Trough Lane, leading north out of Bovey Tracey – the one John Cann would have taken in his flight with the treasure chest – is a 20ft tall ornate iron pipe standing beside the roadway. This is a 'stink pipe' (SX819786), a rare survival from the early days of public sewage systems. In dry periods there was often insufficient water in the sewers to flush them through properly and noxious gasses would build up. These gasses were discharged from the highest point in the sewer system, and to make the smell less troublesome to passers-by, tall pipes were used to disperse the stink into the atmosphere – hence 'stink pipes'. Usually these pipes were plain and utilitarian in appearance, but the one in Trough Lane is highly decorative, which possibly explains its survival.

The Stink Pipe.

BOVEY TRACEY

A Bottle-Kiln?

16
Map Ref
SX824785

Tucked away in a corner of the oldest part of the cemetery in Combe Lane, Bovey Tracey, is an old fashioned gravestone, its inscription now indecipherable. A yew tree has grown, beautifully cut into the shape of a bottle-kiln, completely covering it.

For over 200 years, Bovey Tracey was well known for its pottery, fired in huge brick bottle-kilns, two of which have been retained on the site of one pottery as reminders of a vanished industry.

Are the grave and its bottle-kiln-shaped yew reminders of a past proprietor or of an employee at one of the potteries – a sort of living memorial?

A bottle-kiln?

BRADWORTHY

The Square

Bradworthy has the largest square, not only in Devon, but in the whole country. There are many towns with very broad streets which have a greater area, but here it really is a square. Houses, shops (one, a furniture emporium, occupies nearly the whole south side) and the Old Inn (an ancient coaching inn), surround it on all sides, with streets and lanes leading off it. Although St John's church is not directly on the Square, there is an entrance next to the inn.

The little town is at the centre of rich farming country, and this is what gave birth to the Square. For centuries, a large cattle market was held in the Square, and for cleanliness, the whole area was cobbled, so that the manure and straw could be swept away easily. This has now, unfortunately, been asphalted over.

The market would have needed plenty of water, both for watering the cattle and for washing down; and Bradworthy always had a good supply of spring water; another reason for it growth. An old wood-case hand pump still survives on the south side, and the Lord of the Manor gave a 40ft deep well and pump house for the use of the market, which is now well protected. It had to be deep with all the seepage that would have inevitably occurred!

The Square on a quiet day. The pump house can be seen in the centre.

BRANSCOMBE

St Winifred's Sundial

This charming little twelfth-century church snuggles comfortably in the deep valley and contains many treasures. The eighteenth-century three-decker pulpit, where the lessons were read from the bottom deck, the prayers from the middle and the sermon preached from the top (from where the priest could see who had nodded off!), is almost unique in Devon. Certainly unique in Devon, if not the whole country, is St Winifred's sundial. The south-east buttress of the chancel wall acts as the gnomon, its shadow falling on Roman numerals VI to X, cut laterally onto the chancel wall. The priest who cut these numerals had, of course, to obtain the right time at the equinox and this he could have seen from a scratch dial, the slight remnants of which can be seen on the stone lintel over the bricked-up door into the chancel.

The horizontal sundial reading from 7–10 a.m.

In the churchyard is a grim reminder of smuggling days. The tomb of John Hurley, an excise man, tells that he fell from the cliffs while trying to extinguish a signal fire which was lit to guide in a smuggling boat out at sea.

About a mile inland from St Winifred's is the sixteenth-century Bovey House (SY208903), once the home of the Waldron family, before passing by marriage to the Lords Rolle. An interesting feature is the well which once supplied the house with water; it is 130ft deep and the huge bucket is drawn up by a man wheel, 14ft in diameter. This is a tread wheel where the wheel was turned by a person or animal walking around the wheel's inner face. (The 300ft deep well at Carisbrooke Castle on the Isle of Wight was 'walked' by a donkey). On one side of the well, 30ft down, is a chamber large enough for six men to stand upright; this was a 'priest's hole', although it was allegedly used by smugglers in which to hide contraband.

Bovey House is now a beautiful hotel, in the garden of which is a highly decorated water trough bearing the date 1592.

19

Map Ref
SY202909

BRANSCOMBE

The Hangman's Stone

Just beyond Hangman's Corner, where the road to Beer leaves the A3052, and immediately on the corner to a lane leading to Branscombe, there is a large natural boulder known as the Hangman's Stone. The story has it that a thief with a stolen sheep on the end of a rope, rested against the stone; the sheep in its frantic efforts to escape, entangled the rope around the thief's neck and so strangled him! This explains the name but not the origin of the stone itself. When the main road was but a rough, unfenced track across wild heathland, the stone would have been placed there to indicate to travellers where to turn off for Branscombe. Similar stones can be found at crossroads throughout the country, mostly sarsen or silcretes deposited at the end of the last ice age.

Two hills on the coast near Combe Martin in North Devon, Great Hangman (SS600480) and Little Hangman (SS484480), 1,043ft and 720ft respectively, got their names from a former parish boundary stone and about which exactly the same story was told! A strange coincidence, considering the distance of the two hills.

The Hangman's
Stone.

About half a mile west of the Hangman's Stone, along the main road (A3052), is a semicircular stone seat erected to the memory of Dr Gilbart-Smith (SY195911). Memorial seats are not unusual, but what makes this so is the wording on it: 'On this spot, at half-past nine o'clock, after watching the glorious sunset of August Third, 1904, Thomas Gilbart-Smith, MD, FRCS, fell dead from his bicycle. Thunder and Lightning immediately followed. Thus closed a noble life spent in the service of his fellow men. He never turned his back on duty but faithful to his motto "Dare and Do" remained undaunted to the end.'

The original plaques which carried this inscription also showed Dr Gilbart-Smith standing by his bicycle dressed in a Norfolk jacket and knickerbockers and his profile. These two gun-metal plaques were stolen in 1981 and were replaced with the current plaque.

BRAUNTON

The Great Field

It was the Anglo-Saxons who initially cleared the ground south-west of Braunton and enclosed the area with a thorn hedge, much of which survives today. Then, following the slope of the ground to assist drainage, it was ploughed in sections, or furlongs; these were divided from each other by the 'headlands' where the plough, drawn by as many as eight oxen, was turned. The furlongs were

20
Map Ref
SS475358

subdivided into strips, or 'lands' about 220 yards long and 22 yards wide (about an acre, although many were less). One furrow was left unploughed to divide them, and over time these became low banks, or 'balks'.

The farmers, all freemen who worked the field, would have held varying numbers of strips according to their status, from over 100 to as few as two, although all would have had a fair share of the good, poor, wet or stony ground, hence the apparent haphazard ownership, and all would have worked in common, sharing oxen, etc. according to their capabilities. Every farmer, all of whom lived in the narrow, twisting lanes of Braunton and who had their barns and byres there, would take whatever they grew for their own. It is not thought that this was a 'three field system' as were organised in most parts of the country, for although the whole field was open for grazing once the grain had been carried, all had common rights of grazing over the surrounding ground.

After 1066 William, who owned all land by 'right of conquest', gave it to his followers for 'services rendered'; so, although over the succeeding 300 years the method of agriculture did not change, the Saxon 'freemen' became serfs and had to pay 'rent' to the Lord of the Manor, either in tythes from what they grew or by labour working on the Lord's land. It was many centuries later before the rent was paid with money.

Although several 'common fields' still survive in the country (one is on Hawksridge, near Luppitt (ST180060), changes in ownership, population shift and agricultural practices, meant that most became the enclosed, hedgerow countryside of today. So why was the 'Great Field' not enclosed?

✳   ✳   ✳

The Great Field was owned by three manors and because of the way it was divided, it would have been extremely difficult for any one owner to enclose, not only in practice but in law. Even in comparatively recent times, it was still in multiple ownership. It is recorded that in 1841 that 'Bassett had 76 patches of land, Georges had 65 patches and Courteney had 60 patches'. The number of strips within the Great Field steadily declined from 500 strips with 60 cultivators in 1820, to 140 strips with twelve cultivators in 1975. This number has now declined to five and the land is now being cultivated in large blocks which no longer have the appearance of strips. However, some owners have retained the 'headlands', so the old look is maintained to a limited degree. There are no roads or lanes crossing the Field and only one track, the Broadpath, although there is now the threat of a Braunton bypass cutting across its 360 acres.

The Great Field is both difficult to see and almost impossible to envisage from ground level and there is no high spot from which to view it; however, the 'great hedge' can be followed for most of its length on foot or by bicycle, when the wide, open estuary of the River Taw and the wildness of Braunton Burrows can be appreciated.

The Field is clearly marked on Ordnance Survey maps and a full history of the area can be seen in Braunton Museum.

The Great Field with the Broadpath crossing its centre.

BRIXHAM

The Coffin House

21
Map Ref
SX925561

Fishing and all things maritime were for centuries the lifeblood of the little town of Brixham, which had at one time the fifth most important port in the country. The houses cluster around the quayside, clinging to the steep slopes surrounding the harbour and facing north, are protected from the Channel gales.

Believed to have been constructed in about 1640, the Coffin House is set back from the quayside in King Street, where the land starts to

The Coffin House, with steps to the road above.

rise steeply, with a long, steep flight of stone steps curving up on one side and a narrow alleyway on the other. The constraints imposed by the site contribute to its tall and odd appearance, and from certain angles it does look like a coffin stood on its end.

There is, of course, a story behind the house and its name, but unlike most, this one is true. A well-to-do pillar of the community strongly objected to his daughter's choice of a prospective husband, and he told the young man, in no uncertain terms, that he would rather see him in his coffin than be married to his daughter. The couple got married in spite of his objections and as an act of defiance to his words, had this house built in the shape of a coffin!

Unlike some stories, this one has a happy ending; the father eventually saw the humour of the situation and, admiring their spirit, forgave his daughter and accepted his son-in-law into the family.

The Coffin House is now one of Brixham's most photographed buildings, even though it is not particularly photogenic.

BUCKFASTLEIGH

Squire Cabell's Tomb

All over the country there are stories of huge black dogs with glowing eyes stalking country lanes at night, frightening wayfarers as omens of death or disaster. At Uplyme, in the extreme east of Devon, there is a Black Dog Lane and an inn (now a guesthouse) of the same name, whose strong brew probably fostered the story! It is on Dartmoor, though, where such tales are rife, nowhere more so than around its eastern and southern fringes; here again, there is a possible explanation for them.

In the seventeenth century, Squire Richard Cabell, Lord of the Manor of Brooke, near Buckfast, hunted over the moor with his pack of black hounds, which, although answering to the horn while hunting, did not always hear 'home' so would make their own way back to kennels long after dark. Travellers would tell of meeting these hounds, so giving rise to tales of black dogs. A few of these hounds might well have 'gone wild', killing sheep, etc. so enhancing the stories. Sir Arthur Conan Doyle, while staying with a friend at Park Hill House, near Ipplepen, heard of Cabell and his hounds and used the story as the basis for his book *The Hound of the Baskervilles* – Baskerville, incidentally, being the name of his friend's coachman!

Below: Pavillion over Cabell's tomb.

Inset: Cabell's tomb.

Richard Cabell himself no doubt exercised his right of 'droit de seigneur', but must in fact have been far worse, earning such appellations as 'a man of evil reputation' and 'wicked old Squire Cabell'. When he died in 1677, a huge slab of stone (6ft long and nearly 1ft thick) was placed on top of his tomb 'to keep him down' so that he could not rise and again terrorise the countryside; as an extra precaution, a roofed pavilion was erected over the tomb, having a locked door and a decorated iron grill. The tomb is situated almost opposite the south porch of Buckfast's Holy Trinity Church, which was destroyed by arson in 1992. Strangely, Cabell's tomb was not harmed and already there is a story that the fire was caused by devil worshipers – so are myths born. The spire of Holy Trinity survived and can still be seen rising over the trees on the hill above Buckfast and the Abbey.

Cabell trying to escape through the caves?
(Peter Glanvill)

There is another myth in the making regarding Squire Cabell. The quarries at Buckfast have revealed extensive cave systems which speleologists have explored thoroughly; within the last few years yet another system has been found, going directly underneath Holy Trinity Church. At this point in the cave an unusual and peculiarly shaped stalactite has grown, shaped like a little old man with a prominent chin, hooked nose, short body and outstretched arms. Unable to rise from his tomb due to the weight of the stone on top of his grave, has Cabell now tried to burrow downwards? Luckily, because his legs are fused together, he cannot yet pursue his wicked ways!

BUCKLAND-IN-THE-MOOR

23
Map Ref
SX720730

The Clock Face

William Whitley was the proprietor of a Paignton brewery and Paignton Zoo. In the early part of the twentieth century, he moved to Buckland Court, becoming Lord of the Manor, and in 1930, one of his acts of munificence was to have St Peter's Church repaired and to install a clock in its tower. However, instead of numerals on the clock face, he substituted twelve letters spelling out the words MY DEAR MOTHER. It is thought that William felt guilty for neglecting his mother, and that the clock face was as a visible and public reminder whenever he attended church.

The clock face reads 'My Dear Mother'.

BURGH ISLAND

24
Map Ref
SX648439

Burgh Island and its Tractor

Bigbury Bay stretches from Gara Point to Bolt Tail with, just offshore from Bigbury-on-Sea, the 10-acre Burgh Island, isolated at high tide but connected to the mainland at low tide by acres of firm, fine sand. Until 1930, the island was home to just a few sheep, the ruined chapel of St Michael, a fish store and an inn, The Pilchard. Its north shore being sheltered from the worst weather it provided, no doubt, an alternative landing place for the Bigbury fishermen. (Hence the inn in which to wait for the tide to go out, for fishing was the main occupation – apart from a little smuggling).

All this changed in 1930 when a huge, modern hotel was built on the island, with an additional large wing added in 1934. Today the Burgh Island Hotel retains its glorious Art Deco interior and decorations and is one of Devon's premier hotels. Ever since it was built, it has attracted the great and the good (Agatha Christie loved it and set her novel and play *Evil under the Sun* on the island.)

The violent meeting of the waters off Burgh Island in the 1920s, with the Pilchard Inn and a wooden chalet where the hotel is now.

There was, however, a problem with having a hotel on an island, for although easily accessible at low tide, when the tide came in, from both the west and the east, the tidewaters could become tumultuous and yet not deep enough for a boat to take passengers.

The tractor at
Burgh Island.

The answer was Heath Robinson in appearance but entirely practical – a half-track vehicle with a platform on stilts to carry the engine and passengers high above the water. This lasted until just after the war, when an ex-army 'duck' was used. In 1960 the 'sea tractor' was designed by Robert Jackson and built by Beares of Newton Abbot, but it was not until 1969 that the current third generation sea tractor, the only one like it in the world, became successful. The four huge wheels are driven and steered independently by hydraulic power, with the engine on the passenger platform as it was previously.

To watch the sea tractor coming through the racing tides is like watching a leviathan emerging from the deep – a unique sight, and the ride itself is worth every penny!

There is only one snag with the hotel itself – to look at this building is glorious, but its view north overlooks the rash of bungalows that is Bigbury-on-Sea and the serried ranks of caravans at Challaborough.

CHELFHAM

The Viaduct

Driving up the long, wooded ascent from Barnstaple to Bratton Fleming and Exmoor, on rounding one of the many corners, there on the right, near the hamlet of Chelfham, is a railway viaduct – all up there!

The long war between Britain and France at the beginning of the nineteenth century drastically curtailed foreign travel, with the town and villages around England's coasts taking quick advantage of this. Lynton and Lynmouth became known as the 'English Alps by the Sea', but did not prosper as other seaside towns because for a long time, it had no railway to bring in the visitors – they had to make the final stage by coach or carrier.

The very nature of the terrain between Lynton and Barnstaple, the nearest main station, meant that a standard gauge line was impractical. There were many proposals but eventually it was decided to build a 19½ mile long narrow-gauge (1ft 11½in) line from Barnstaple, financed largely by Sir George Newnes, the publisher, who lived at

Lynton. Because the line was narrow-gauge, the engineering works would cost less, but were nevertheless daunting, for the line had to rise from sea level to well over 900ft before descending to Lynton – even then the terminus was a mile from the town and 400ft above it! It opened in 1898 and closed in 1935, after having been taken over by the Southern Railway in 1923, not being the financial success that was envisaged. Because of the remote countryside through which the line passed, and the even more remote stretches of Exmoor, a great deal of the line can still be traced; it just hasn't been worth anyone's effort to remove the bridges or fill in the cuttings. The railway station buildings at Blackmoor Gate are recognisable as such, even though they are now a cafe/restaurant, though the Lynton & Barnsataple Railway's greatest engineering feat, the eight-arched brick viaduct crossing the Stoke Rivers valley at Chelfham, remains as the line's lasting memorial.

Had the line survived until after the war, it would undoubtedly be a major tourist attraction now, for it passed through glorious countryside affording stupendous views of moor and sea.

CHERITON FITZPAINE

School in a Longhouse

26
Map Ref
SS867060

The primary school in Cheriton Fitzpaine is in a building probably older than any other school in the county, if not the country. The building was a traditional, seventeenth-century thatched longhouse (possibly originally the Church House) and the old semicircular oven can still be seen where the building backs on to the churchyard. It was first recorded as a school in 1642, when there was a 'School Chamber' within the house – the pillared extension built out over the high pavement – later also becoming a workhouse.

In 1833 there were two public day schools (parents paying a few pence per child), and these amalgamated in 1850, continuing to use the School Chamber until it became a Board School in 1870 (i.e. having a 'board of governors' comprised usually of local worthies, including the squire, and vicar). Devon County Council took it over in 1903 when it became Cheriton Fitzpaine Council School, with the schoolhouse being converted into extra school accommodation in 1983.

Longhouse School from the churchyard. Note the bread oven.

As the school backs directly onto the churchyard, it has never been able to develop in that direction, and there are now plans to build a new school on another site in the village.

27

Map Ref
ST163141

CLAYHIDON

The Murderer's Stone

Far up the remote valley of the River Culm, near the charmingly named hamlet of Rosemary Lane, a neat cast-iron plate stands in the hedge beside the road. It reads 'Wm Blackmore Land Surveyor, of

Clayhidon Mills was murdered on this spot the 6th Day of February 1853 by George Sparks of this parish who was executed at Exeter for this horid crime'. The story behind this is prosaic enough. Blackmore went to collect money from a farmer, John Honeyball, a transaction witnessed by two of Honeyball's men, George Sparks and a man named Hitchcock. Sparks and Hitchcock went drinking that night at the White Horse Inn at Bolham and again met Blackmore; at 1 a.m. they left the inn together, laughing and talking amicably. However, after Hitchcock had gone his separate way, Sparks hit Blackmore with a pair of heavy tongs he had been carrying, killing him before taking his money. Sparks was arrested, tried and then, on a new scaffold, executed at Exeter Gaol before a crowd of 12,000. What makes this commemorative plate so unusual is that either the parish or Blackmore's friends and relatives felt the need, at no little cost, to remember the event in such a permanent manner. After all, murder for gain was not uncommon and was rarely commemorated in such a public fashion.

CLOVELLY

No Through Traffic

28
Map Ref
SY317247

To say that the village of Clovelly is unique is an understatement, for as Barbara Cherry and Nikolaus Pevsner state in their book *Devon*, 'it is quite beyond description'.

There are two distinct areas to Clovelly – the harbour and the village itself. The harbour was built in 1587 by George Carey, Lord of the Manor, and for centuries had a large and flourishing herring fishing fleet. It also afforded the only shelter for shipping along the open and dangerous coast between Padstow and Ilfracombe, that is, if Bideford is discounted because of the treacherous bar at the mouth of the River Taw.

The prosperous fishing industry resulted in a growth of population and the need for housing. Any level ground near the harbour had long been utilised, so the only way was up through the wooded cliffs, which were far too steep for any road or street. The answer was to build a street of steps, the inn and houses along each side having their doorsteps almost on a level with the roofs of the houses below, with an occasional side alley. Carrying goods posed no problems – packhorses had been the commonest method of transport for centuries, and donkeys with their creels were also a way of life in fishing villages. Sledges had also been in use on upland farms in place of wheeled carts, and these were frequently used, for they could be slid down over the steps, a donkey restraining them from behind, and could easily be pulled up when empty. Adaptations are still in use today with the donkey as an added visitor attraction.

High Street,
Clovelly, c. 1930.

The Hamlyns, who succeeded the Careys as lords of the manor, realised the visitor potential and did much to retain the charm of the area. A new road, The Hobby, was constructed, running for 2 miles from Hobby Lodge on the A39 (SY338232) to the top of the village, winding above the wooded cliffs and affording stupendous sea views. Due to the foresight of Mrs Christine Hamlyn, who died in 1936, the character of the village was retained, with strict controls over any developments and alterations to frontages along the street.

Clovelly now has a large car park and visitor centre, sited well back from the top so visitors can walk down the steps to the harbour (and back again if they so want or are able to do so!) There is a shuttle service of busses running to and from the centre, down a new road to the west of the village, over which, with very few exceptions, other motor vehicles are strictly prohibited.

29
Map Ref
SY254926

COLYFORD

Cast-Iron Urinal

The single-track branch railway from Seaton Junction to Seaton (opened in 1868) had a halt at Colyford, but after the Beeching Report closed the line in the 1960s, the section of line between Seaton and Colyton became a tourist attraction as a tramline with historic trams; this, however, necessitated the platforms being lowered. Now stranded high and dry on the original level of the old platform is that once familiar essential feature, a cast-iron urinal. This rare survivor now stands as a stark reminder of the railway age, when everything was provided for the convenience of travellers.

Inaccessible!

COLYTON

A Protective Wall

Colyton House is bounded along Vicarage Street by a very high wall – over 20ft – which has a rather sad story of unrequited love. When early in the nineteenth century, the owner brought his young and beautiful bride to Colyton House, he became intensely jealous of her being seen walking in the grounds, especially by one particular young man who lived in Berry House opposite. The jealous husband had the existing low wall raised to its present height, so that even from the upper windows of Berry House, his garden could not be seen and thereby his wife was made safe from prying eyes. The young man, however, was not to be thwarted and had an extra floor built onto his house, enabling him once again to overlook the garden of Colyton House and see his inamorata. Frustratingly, the story ends here, as nothing is known of the final outcome. Perhaps the young man tired of seeing the object of his affection from afar (or found a more approachable young lady!), for the extra floor at Berry House remained incomplete and empty for many years, and only in 1996 was it made habitable.

Below, left: The High Wall can be seen on the right-hand side.

Below, right: Max's grave.

31
Map Ref
SS580460

The garden of Colyton House provides another sentimental story. Under a great Holm Oak on the lawn of the house is a large, flat gravestone inscribed MAX MDCCCLXXIV (1874) followed by, in classical Greek capitals, a quotation taken from the Epistle to the Romans, Chapter 8, Verses 20–21. Its literal translation reads, 'In hope that the creature itself also shall be delivered'. Max must have been a much-loved pet.

COMBE MARTIN

The Pack o'Cards

During the eighteenth century, gambling was rife among the gentry, with huge sums of money changing hands on the turn of a card or a throw of a dice; when gamblers lost, they often lost their property, but when they made a spectacular win they liked to proclaim the fact in a way that all could see.

George Ley, a North Devon landowner, won a large sum of money playing cards and celebrated this win by building a new house for himself in Combe Martin in honour of his favourite pastime. Built like a child's house of cards, it had four floors representing the four suits, with each floor having thirteen rooms and thirteen doors, and

The Pack o'Cards.

the whole house having fifty-two windows. Some of these windows were subsequently blocked up in 1784 because of the window tax brought in by William Pitt the Younger (these bricked-up windows became known as 'Pitt's Pictures').

The Leys eventually sold the house and it became an inn called the King's Arms, later becoming the most unusual and best known public house in Devon – the Pack o'Cards.

There is an interesting story of an old table chest at the inn with a false top, which, when lifted, revealed a space large enough to hide three men. This provided a quick, accessible hiding place from the press-gangs who scoured the countryside, especially the ports, forcing able-bodied men to serve in the Navy. It could, of course, have equally served as a convenient hiding place for any illicit liquor brought in by smugglers.

In the eighteenth century, William Northmore, MP for Okehampton, who lived at Wonson Manor, near Throwleigh, lost £17,000 on the turn of a card – the ace of diamonds. To remind him of his folly he had the ace of diamonds painted in red onto the panelled wall of his living room. It is still there but today is hidden from view!

COPPLESTONE

The Copp Stone

32
Map Ref
SS770025

The square, 106in-high granite Copp Stone stands in the centre of the forked junction where the road from Barnstaple (A377) meets the road from Okehampton (A3072). It is covered from top to bottom with early Celtic interlacing carvings, with the badly worn carving of a man on horseback (possibly Bishop Putta) at the top of one side and

The Copp Stone.

three empty niches on the others, once possibly having held figures. What makes this Dark Ages stone particularly interesting is that this form of Celtic interlaced work is only found elsewhere in the far north of England, and being granite, must have been extremely difficult to carve.

The term Dark Ages applies to that period in history between the fifth and eleventh centuries, which were 'darkened' by the lack of contemporary written sources, and this is certainly true of the Copp Stone.

Putta, Bishop of Hereford, was journeying between Crediton and North Tawton when he was attacked and murdered; a memorial to him – the Copp Stone – was erected in AD 905 at the

crossroads near to the site if the attack (SS750048). A Charter of King Edgar (943–75) in AD 474 stated that anyone moving the stone would be 'stricken with a perpetual curse and perish everlastingly with the Devil, unless he shows by reparation to make atonement'. Whether this was before or after it was moved 2 miles down the road to its present site is not mentioned.

It seems likely that the village of Copplestone took its name from the Copp Stone, having added 'le' to the spelling. However, there was an old Devon family with a similar name (see p. 107) but with only one 'p', of which it was said:

> Crocker, Cruwys and Coplestone
> When the Conqueror came were found at home

Did this family take their name from the village, the Copp Stone, or was it the other way round?

33
Map Ref
SS834001

CREDITON

War Memorial

All too often memorials to the fallen are rather unprepossessing stone monoliths tucked away near the parish church, and only on special occasions of private or public remembrance are they looked at closely. However, in the main street of Crediton, near a small public garden, the war memorial is not only a handsome and imaginative piece of architecture, but it is also functional.

The stone, on which are inscribed the names of those who died for their country, is placed centrally under an open, eight-sided tiled roof, the whole of which is surmounted by a tall, graceful tiled spire. Around the stone is a seat where people can rest or talk. Sheltered from the elements, locals, both young and old, use it as a rendezvous and it also acts as a useful reference point.

Crediton is an old town with a glorious church, the Holy Cross, and a diverse wealth of architecture, which the memorial complements.

CULLOMPTON

If you want to know the time . . .

34
Map Ref
SY020074

The tall, imposing building in the Square with its clock, now known as the Town Clock, was built in 1898 as the East Devon Headquarters of the Devonshire Constabulary, as can be seen from the inscription around the clock face. Then, as now, the police wanted their presence known – where better than in the centre of the town – and they had their coat of arms cut in stone over the door of the Police House (ST272019).

The Cullompton policemen were men of many parts, and had only to change their blue helmets for brass ones, and their 'beetle-crushers' for calf-length leather boots to double up as firemen. The police station at Cullompton also doubled as the town's fire station, hence the fire bell at the top of the building. The horse-drawn steam pump was kept behind the double doors on the right (now replaced by a window) and the two horses were kept in a field and stables at the rear of the station building. Nothing remains of the original interior for it is an estate agent's office – the licked pencil stubs replaced by computer screens!

Above: Police clock and fire bell.

Left: Old Police House at Membury showing the Devon Constabulary coat of arms.

35
Map Ref
ST103135

CULMSTOCK

A High Yew

Richard Doddridge Blackmore (1825–1900) grew up in the village of Culmstock, where his father was curate-in-charge of the parish. Although R.D. Blackmore is better known as the author of *Lorna Doone* (1869), he also wrote other romantic novels depicting scenes of rural life in east Devon and village worthies drawn from people he knew in his boyhood. *Perlycross* (1894), for example, is set around Culmstock. In it, he mentions a little yew tree growing out of the top of the tower of All Saints Church, thereby placing the yew's age at between 200 and 300 years old. Having been starved of nutriment and having its root system severely curtailed for all those years, it has grown stunted, as do Japanese bonsai. It says a lot for the construction of the tower that the yew's roots haven't split the fabric.

DARTMOOR

The Coffin Stone

Ecclesiastical custom had decreed that every burial must take place in the deceased's own parish, thus, as the Forest of Dartmoor lies wholly within the parish of Lydford, anyone living (and dying) on the moor had to be buried there. In the days before roads were built across the moor, carrying a coffin across miles of inhospitable moorland was a back-breaking and gruelling undertaking for the relatives and neighbours of the deceased, especially during winter. In the thirteenth century, Walter Bronscombe, Bishop of Exeter, made a special dispensation to those who lived on the eastern side of Dartmoor that they could bury their dead at Widecombe; although no longer having to cross the high moor, it remained, nevertheless, a daunting task.

Over the years, it became traditional to put the coffin down at certain places so that the bearers could rest and have refreshment. During the steep climb up from Dartmeet, where the cortège would have crossed the East Dart River by the clapper bridge, there was a large, flat granite boulder on which the coffin could be rested, and which, over the centuries, became known as the Coffin Stone. The crosses and initials of those to be buried were cut into the rock at the time by the bearers, and although now much worn, can still be made

The Coffin Stone showing a cross and initial.
(© Glen Bearne www.dartmoor-crosses.org.uk)

out. There is also a large crack across the stone, which, as the story goes, was caused by a lightning bolt striking it after the body of a wicked man had been rested on it! The B3357 now winds up the hill on an easier route than the old track, so the Coffin Stone is now to the west of the road.

There can be no doubt that during severe weather, burials had to be delayed for days or even weeks, and there is a (probably) apocryphal story about one such incident. During dreadful weather, a traveller managed to get as far as the old New House Inn (now the Warren House Inn) and was given a room for the night. On retiring, he found an old chest in his room, which, when opened, revealed a corpse. Suspecting murder, the man rushed down to tell the landlord, who placidly said 'it was old feyther' and explained that as the weather was too bad to take him to Lydford, 'us salted un down'! Most farms had vats in which bacon could be salted down, so there is possibly some truth in the story.

Adjoining the thatched Church House and leading to the beautiful little granite built church of St Mary at Throwleigh (SX667907), is a thatched lych-gate. While the priest receives the body and recites the first prayer for the burial of the dead, the coffin is usually placed on trestles. Here, however, in the centre of the lych-gate under the thatch, is a dressed block of granite on which to rest the coffin. Is this continuing a long tradition?

DARTMOOR

37
Map Ref
SX732799

Jay's Grave

At the beginning of the nineteenth century, Kitty Jay was a workhouse orphan working as a skivvy on a Manaton farm; when she was sixteen she was seduced by the son of the farmer, became pregnant and in despair, hanged herself in a barn.

Since suicides were forbidden a Christian burial in a churchyard, Kitty was buried, as was custom, at a crossroad, where a track to Hedge Barton led off the road from Swine Down to Heatree Cross; this was where the parishes of Manaton, Widecombe and North Bovey met, so none would have responsibility for her grave. Over the years, the story went around that only a sheep was buried there, so in about 1860, the owner of Hedge Barton, James Bryant, had the grave opened and a doctor confirmed that the skeleton was indeed

Jay's grave.

that of a young woman. Bryant had her re-interred in a wooden coffin, with a raised grave surrounded by granite stones, with a larger one at Kitty's head – and there the grave remains today.

But who regularly placed the flowers on poor Kitty's grave? These first appeared in about 1900 with that great local character and lover of the moor, Olive Katherine Parr, better known as the author Beatrice Chase, or, as she liked to be called, 'My Lady of the Moor'. It was she who regularly filled a jam jar with seasonal flowers and greenery, and when she died in 1955, others carried on the tradition. Beatrice Chase loved the mysteries and folk stories connected with the moor and unconsciously created another.

Half a mile across the moor, to the east, is the 18ft high natural rock on Hayne Down known as Bowerman's Nose (SX741804). Worn by time and weather, the rock has a remarkable likeness to a man's head, with a large nose and wearing a cardinal's hat! Prosaically, the name stems from the Celtic, Bowerman being 'vawr maen' – the great stone. The addition of 'Nose' is of more recent origin.

Bowerman's Nose, Dartmoor.

Such a distinctive feature on the landscape has gathered stories as to how it came by that name. One was that a huntsman, called Bowerman, rode his pack of hounds through a coven of witches who had gathered on Hayne Down. This so annoyed them that when next he hunted in the neighbourhood, one of the witches turned herself into a hare (a favourite trick of witches). Bowerman set his hounds on it, hunting it to Hayne Down, where the witches buried him up to his neck before turning him into stone. His hounds received the same treatment and now form nearby Hound Tor.

The rock did not escape the attention of the Romantic poets of the early nineteenth century, for N.T. Carrington (1777–1830) included the following in his *Dartmoor: A Descriptive Poem*:

> On the very edge
> Of the vast moorland, startling every eye,
> A shape enormous rises! High it towers
> Above the hill's bold brow, and seen from far,
> Assumes the human form; a granite god, –
> To whom in days long flown, the suppliant knee
> In trembling homage bowed. The hamlets near
> Have legends rude connected with the spot,
> (Wild swept by every wind) on which he stands
> The giant of the Moor!

DARTMOOR

38
Map Ref
SX658728

Jolly Lane Cott

Halfway up the steep and twisting Jolly Lane, leading up from the old Huccaby Bridge over the West Dart River to Hexworthy, there is an unremarkable-looking stone cottage on the right-hand side. It might be unexceptional to look at, but it signifies the ending of an old custom – almost an unwritten law.

It had been a custom throughout the country that if a house could be built and roofed in one day then that house and the land on which it

stood became the inalienable property of the builder. All over the country can be seen houses with long narrow gardens beside the road – built probably on the wide verge where once cattle or sheep were herded.

Jolly Lane Cott was the last such house to be built. In 1835, Tom and Sally Satterley decided that the only way they could escape bonded employment was to build a home of their own. Near midsummer's day when the working day was the longest, Tom and Sally, with their friends, relatives and neighbours, set to work and built it. It was the last time that this right was exercised, for shortly afterwards the right was extinguished in law so no more could be built in this way.

Sally must have been a practical woman for it is said that she could shoe a horse, thatch a roof and build a stone wall as well as any man. She survived her husband by many years and on her death in 1901, she was honoured by a moor-man's 'carrying funeral' to the churchyard at Widecombe.

Just above the cottage, directly adjoining the lane, are the roofless remains of a tiny granite structure, the stone lintel of the doorway being barely 5ft above the sill and the shell of an open fireplace still in one corner of the single downstairs room. Was this the 'home' from which Tom and Sally escaped in 1835?

DARTMOOR

The Ten Commandments Stones

William Whitley was the proprietor of a Paignton brewery and of Paignton Zoo, moving in the early part of the twentieth century to Buckland Court. In 1925, it was proposed that the Book of English Prayer should be revised and that a New Book of Common Prayer be introduced, favouring Anglo-Catholicism; although this was accepted by the House of Lords, it was twice rejected by the House of Commons. This proposed changing of the Prayer Book had so incensed Whitley, that when the Bill was thrown out, he wanted to celebrate the fact. He owned Buckland Beacon, a 1,287ft-tall granite tor commanding views over Dartmoor, the valley of the River Dart and South Devon; an admirable place for a memorial.

In 1928, Whitley chose two natural boulders at the base of the tor and engaged W. Arthur Clement, a stonemason from Exmouth, to dress them and inscribe on them the dates when the Bill was defeated (15.12.1927 and 14.06.1928) alongside the Ten Commandments. Also added was the Eleventh Commandment from John, Chapter 13, Verse 34: 'A new commandment I give unto you, That ye love one another; as I have loved you, that ye also love one another', and the third verse of O God, Our Help in Ages Past to fill up the space left.

Living in a hut in the woods, Clement commenced his task on 23 July and completed it on 31 August. He finished up looking like a moor-man – wild and bearded, and Whitley, on a visit, told him 'Twill call you Moses', to which Clement replied that Moses carried the tablets down, which he felt unable to do!

The inscribed words are now becoming worn but are still readable and remain as a relic of the Commons defeat.

DARTMOUTH

40
Map Ref
SX875521

HMS Britannia

The flooded river-valley through which the River Dart flows in its final 10 miles before joining the open sea through a narrow, rocky channel, provided a deep and safe anchorage for shipping, especially later when the narrow mouth was guarded by Kingswear and Dartmouth Castles.

It is hardly surprising therefore that Dartmouth has as long a maritime and naval history as any town in the country. In the twelfth century, Richard Coeur de Lion sailed from Dartmouth in 'one hundred ships and fourteen busses' for the First Crusade to the Holy Land; in 1347 the town provided thirty-one ships for the siege of Calais, and in 1588 sent many boats to defend the Channel from the Spanish Armada. After Sir Francis Drake 'had singed the King of Spain's beard' with the capture of the richly-laden caraque, the *San Philip*, he brought it back to Dartmouth to share the booty with his crew and Queen Elizabeth I.

Commercially, a thriving wine trade was developed with Portugal, and Dartmouth had the foremost of the fishing fleets which sailed to the Newfoundland banks. When, however, the breakwater was built in Plymouth Sound, so providing a much larger and safer anchorage, Dartmouth's importance as a port for the Navy declined drastically.

HMS *Britannia* at Dartmouth, 1905.

The Britannia, Dartmouth.

In 1863 the 73-year-old, wooden three-decker man-of-war, HMS *Britannia*, together with another ship, the *Hindustan* (later replaced by the *Prince Albert* in 1869) were moored permanently in the river off Sandquay, in which to train officer cadets for the Royal Navy. In 1900, land belonging to the Raleigh estate above the town, was purchased as a site for a new Royal Naval College. Designed by Sir George Aston Webb (who was also responsible for Admiralty Arch in London), it was opened in 1905 as the Royal Naval College, HMS *Britannia* (for all naval shore establishments are ships). In 1943, the cadets had to leave, for the college became the base for Combined Operations, known as HMS Dartmouth III and later renamed HMS Effingham. It was at Dartmouth that the landing-craft used in training for amphibious landings on Slapton Sands (see p. 124) were based. On 5 and 6 July 1944, 485 craft left Dartmouth for the beaches of Normandy.

After the Second World War, the college reverted to its former use and the town became a haven for small boats and yachtsmen.

DEVONSHIRE

41

Devonshire Epitaphs

Epitaphs found on old tombs and gravestones not only tell us something of those buried there, but also of the mores of days gone by when people dealt with death in a more open fashion – the heartbreak at the death of a child, rustic humour – often by the use of puns, or with dire warnings of the reader's own mortality. There are many to be found in Devon's churches and graveyards, but here is a small selection.

In the churchyard of St Gregory's at Seaton, a stone commemorates John Starre, of Beer, with an incised star and these lines:

> Starre on Hie!
> Where should a star be
> But on Hie?
> Tho underneath he now doth lie
> Sleeping in dust
> Yet shall he rise
> More glorious than
> Starres in the Skies.

St Michael's at Loddiswell has a memorial to two young women, Katherine Wood and Anne Furzeland, who died on the same day in 1665. Someone could not resist, in commemorating their lives, by ending thus: 'How soon does green Wood shrink and Furzeland waste. And turn to ashes with death's flaming blast'.

The almost libellous epitaph at St Michael's, Bideford, remembers a particular lady whose character was obviously very well known, as was the lady's buried next to her:

> Here lies the body of Mary Sexton
> Who pleased many a man, but ne'er vext'd one,
> Not like the woman who lies under the next stone.

One wonders if this was written by the husband of the lady, but who also knew Mary well!

Set on a stone in the floor of the chancel of St Winifred's, Branscombe, are the sad words telling of the death of Anne Bartlett in 1609:

> Here lieth a blossom of the world's great tree
> Who was as fair as buds of roses be.
> She died an infant, Heaven was made for such.
> Live like an infant, thou shall have as much.

Even more poignant is the epitaph to Samuel Kidwell, aged 11 months, in the churchyard at Tawstock:

> He tasted of life's bitter cup,
> Refused to drink the potions up;
> But turned his little head aside,
> Disgusted with the taste – and died.

In the tower of St Petrock's at Petrockstow, a tablet commemorates the life of a much-loved wife who died in 1810:

> She was –
> But words are wanting to say what:
> Think what a wife should be
> And she was that.

A stone in the Church of St Mary and St Peter at Salcombe Regis records the end of an ancient and respected family at the close of the eighteenth century:

> See, see, spectator and behold
> Whether you're young or whether you're old
> What you in time must be.
> For strength nor beauty cannot save,
> Nor wealth protect you from the grave;
> You shall be dust like me.

Inscribed on a gravestone in the churchyard of St Petrock, Lydford, is this fulsome eulogy:

> Here lies in horizontal position
> The Outside case of
> GEORGE ROUTLEIGH, Watchmaker
> Whose abilities in that line were an honour
> To his profession
> Integrity was the mainspring,
> And prudence the regulator
> Of all the actions of his life.
> Human, generous and liberal
> His hand never stopped
> Till he had relieved distress.
> So much regulated were his motions
> That he never went wrong
> Except when set agoing
> By people
> Who did not know his key.
> Even then he was easily
> Set right again.
> He had the art of disposing his time
> So well
> That his hours glided away
> In one continual round
> Of pleasure and delight
> Till an unlucky moment put a period to
> His existence.
> He departed this life
> Nov 14 1802
> Aged 57
> Wound up
> In hopes of being taken in hand
> By his Maker
> And of being thoroughly cleaned, repaired
> And set-going
> In the world to come.

Robert Phillips, a Kingsbridge cooper, herbalist, and, according to a contemporary, 'a drunken old vagabond', was fond of telling anyone who would listen what he had written as his epitaph and where it was to be placed. When he died in 1795, this was duly carried out and positioned near the priest's door of St Edmund's Church, so becoming one of the best known and oft-quoted epitaphs in the country:

> Here I lie at the Chancel door,
> Here I lie because I'm poor;
> The farther in, the more you'll pay,
> Here I am as warm as they.

Another equally famous epitaph can be found in St George's Church, Dean Prior, where Robert Herrick was the vicar between 1654 and 1674. Herrick, one of the great English poets, had a love/hate relationship with Devonshire, which came across in many of his poems, but he was unequivocal about his feelings for his maid, 'kind Prew'. He was with her when she died and penned these lines to her memory:

> In this little urn is laid
> Prewdence Baldwin (once my maid):
> From whose happy spark here let
> Spring the purple violet.

In the Church of St Nicholas and St Cyriacus at South Pool can be found a very worn fourteenth-century effigy of Muriel Courtney, wife of an Earl of Devon. The words alone are delightful, but to fully appreciate them, the effigy should be seen:

> Here lies a most beautiful lady
> Light of step and heart was she
> I think she was the most beautiful lady
> That ever was in the West Country

No list of epitaphs should omit one for a pet. In the days when railway stations had carefully tended flowerbeds, there was often a resident cat. When the one belonging to Lustleigh Station, on the Newton Abbot to Moretonhampstead line died, it was buried beside the track near its favourite flowerbed, and a stone was erected bearing these simple words:

> Beneath this stone, and laid out flat
> Lies Jumbo, once our station cat.

Alas, the stone was a victim of Dr Beeching when the lines were taken up in the 1960s.

DEVONSHIRE

42

Crossing Dry–shod

Beckford Bridge (ST265014) over the River Yarty, near Membury, is typical of the packhorse bridges throughout the country, used in the days when the packhorse was the commonest form of transporting goods. Even after the use for which it had been made became outdated, there was still a ford to cross, and those on foot made good use of it until the ford was culverted in the 1930s. It is now a scheduled monument.

Thomas Moore in his *History of Devonshire* (1829) wrote: 'Fifty years ago a pair of wheels was scarcely to be seen on a farm in the county [!] and at present the use of packhorses still prevails . . . hay, corn, fuel, dung, stone, lime, etc. and the products of the fields are all conveyed on horseback with packsaddles or strakes.' So, except on the main roads, bridges to carry vehicular traffic were unnecessary and it was only drovers or travellers on foot who had to keep their feet dry, for unless carrying wool or salt, the packhorses could splash across, particularly on Dartmoor. The 'great roads' across the moor – from Plymouth to Moretonhampstead and Tavistock to Ashburton – were not completed until about 1770.

The narrow bridges built for the packhorse or foot traveller were built with materials easy to come by, and on Dartmoor, that meant granite – slabs of moor stone which had only to be roughly dressed. Although extremely heavy to move, once in position, their very weight made them secure and safe from floodwaters.

Beckford Bridge.

An old man on the Walla Brook.

Where the stream was narrow, then a single slab would suffice, such as the one over the Walla Brook (SX654872). To span a broader river, however, several slabs placed end-to-end were needed with piers to support them; these were also of loose blocks with only the weight of the 'bridge' holding them firm. The finest of these clapper bridges can be found at Postbridge (SX647788), with two piers supporting the central span of two massive slabs set side by side, each measuring 15ft × 6ft and weighing many tons. The sheer effort of moving and positioning them is hard to imagine, given the limited resources available in those early days.

Around the fringes of the moor where granite was not so readily accessible, the packhorse bridges were of more traditional design, although not so finely constructed as elsewhere in the county. Saddle Horse Bridge (SX779801) is a splendid example and crosses the River Bovey beside a ford on the long-disused road from Gradnor Bridge, near Lustleigh, before it climbs up on to Trendlebere Down. Although not signposted, this charming little bridge in its woodland setting with its cobbled surface is well worth the walk for a picnic.

Postbridge, Dartmoor.

Even when roads became fit for wheeled traffic, there were still fords to cross and the feet of travellers to keep dry, so a footbridge was necessary. Old ways die hard and many footbridges were simply slabs of stone. A good example of this can be found on the Ilsington road, just east of Cold East Cross (SX744888). The ford was replaced by a concrete bridge in the 1920s, and just downstream, spanning a narrow channel, is the old footbridge – two slabs of granite placed side by side.

However, the oldest way of all to cross a river was by stepping-stones, so they deserve a mention; the problem with these is deciding which were placed conveniently in position by nature, and which had a little help from man. The best of the latter can be found crossing the West Dart at Dartmeet, just above its confluence with the East Dart (SX671730).

Saddle Horse
Bridge over the
River Bovey.

Cold East Cross.

A tricky crossing
of the East Dart at
Dartmeet.

DEVONSHIRE

43

Pub Names

In populated areas, public houses and inns were often named after a local trade or occupation, a locality, or in honour of a famous personage of the time. In the countryside, more often than not, ale or cider was sold from a private house or farm, and it wasn't until the eighteenth century that a building was employed specifically for the sale of drink and given a name – hence the plethora of 'New Inns' at that time. Devon, as the third largest county in the country, has hundreds of pubs and inns, and some very curious names with interesting histories can be found.

The Jack Russell (SY619298) at Swimbridge, near Barnstaple, commemorates both a famous local hunting parson and the breed of dog named after him. John (Jack) Russell came across a small dog which he thought would make a good hunt 'terrier' – a dog small enough to get into a fox's earth to make it bolt. From that one dog came a line of terriers – Jack Russells – which today are one of the most popular breeds, for besides being brave and strong hearted, they also make delightful, loyal pets.

There is no doubt as to how the isolated Warren House Inn (SX674809) got its name, for it was close to a large 'warren' or 'bury' where rabbits were bred in artificial burrows. The inn was formerly called the New House Inn and was sited on the opposite side of the B3212 road to its current position, catering for the miners who worked the nearby tin deposits. When self-styled poet Jonas Coaker became landlord in the nineteenth century, he had this building demolished and rebuilt it on the other side of the road. Why he did this is a mystery, for the New House Inn was on common ground so he paid no rent, but the opposite side was owned by the Duchy of Cornwall who, naturally, exacted a rent.

The Warren House Inn is the highest public house in southern England at 1,450ft above sea level, and the third highest in the country, with Tan Hill in the Yorkshire Dales being the highest at 1,800ft. Tradition has it that since the Warren House Inn was built the fire in the bar has never been allowed to go out.

How the Nobody Inn (SX836867) at Doddiscombsleigh got such an odd name is simple in the extreme. Many years ago, the innkeeper and his family were in the habit of frequently visiting Exeter and leaving the inn open and unattended, with the customers free to draw their own drinks and leaving the money for them on the bar – because there was nobody in!

In the early 1950s, the landlord of the New Inn (SX518800) near Mary Tavey, was one Charles Ossington; Charles was extremely overweight and, because of his size, used to sit on a dais behind the small bar from where he could serve his customers without moving from his seat. One day a friend came into the pub and remarked, 'You look just like an elephant sitting on a nest!' Charles was so tickled by the remark that he changed the pub's name from the New Inn to the Elephant's Nest.

No one seems to know how the remote inn at Challacombe, Exmoor, came to be called the Black Venus (SY674410). One story is that the innkeeper had a pet black sheep; another is that there was once a local breed of sheep of that name, and yet another – by far the most romantic although the most unlikely is that the inn was once kept by a Dutch princess from the East Indies, which would certainly have made an impression in that remote corner of the moor. However, it would be nice to think that an innkeeper from around 1810 had been to London and seen Saartjie Baartman, better known as the Hottentot Venus, performing on stage. On his return to Challacombe his stories of her considerable and ample charms would have ensured good business for months and so given the inn its name.

These are but a flavour of some of the unusual names that can be found by the thirsty traveller in Devon.

DEVONSHIRE

44

The Admiralty Telegraph

At a time when Napoleon was posing a very real danger to this country with a threat of invasion, it was imperative that the Admiralty in London be in close and quick contact with the Naval bases at Portsmouth and Plymouth. So a line of visual signalling stations was built, first from London to Portsmouth, and later extended to Plymouth in 1806.

The stations were roughly 6–10 miles apart, each being visible to the next, and were continually manned during daylight hours. There were two 'lookouts', each having a telescope permanently trained on the adjoining stations, and a 'signaller' who operated the shutters – the telegraph – on the roof above. There were six shutters in two blocks of three set side by side, painted white with a black circle in the centre; these were opened and closed by ropes from within the building, each letter of the alphabet having its own sequence of open and closed shutters. As each combination was read by the receiving lookout he would pass this orally to the signaller for him to retransmit forward. It is said that a message could be sent from Plymouth to London in 20 minutes! The great drawback to this system was that it could not operate at night or in poor weather conditions and was easily blown down in high winds. When the emergency was over the line to Plymouth was closed in 1814, although the London–Portsmouth line continued using the more efficient semaphore system.

No physical remains of the line survive in Devon, but because of the unusual nature of the operation, several names have endured. A cottage on Dalwood Common is still called Telegraph Cottage (SY221009); the steep road from Exeter to the top of Haldon Hill remains as Telegraph Hill (SX910830) and a hill near South Knighton continues to be Telegraph Hill on the present-day maps (SX808732). The site of the stations on St Syrus (St Ceres) hill, just north of Honiton (ST145026), and Lambert's Castle (SY371990) are approximately known, although the one near Rockbeare and the three leading to Fort Wise in Plymouth have yet to be identified.

Such novel constructions, prominently crossing the rural heart of the West Country, must have made a great impression, as would the speed at which news could be sent; the local newspapers taking full advantage of this. The *Sherborne Mercury* of 21 September 1807 reported, 'The Telegraph was at work Wednesday afternoon and brought a message to the Port Admiral [of Plymouth], in fifteen minutes, from London, with the agreeable intelligence of the surrender of Copenhagen and its dependencies . . .' In March 1809 it was reported '. . . the Admiralty semaphore system was very quick, as Capt. Lord Cochrane could testify. On the 19th March he came into

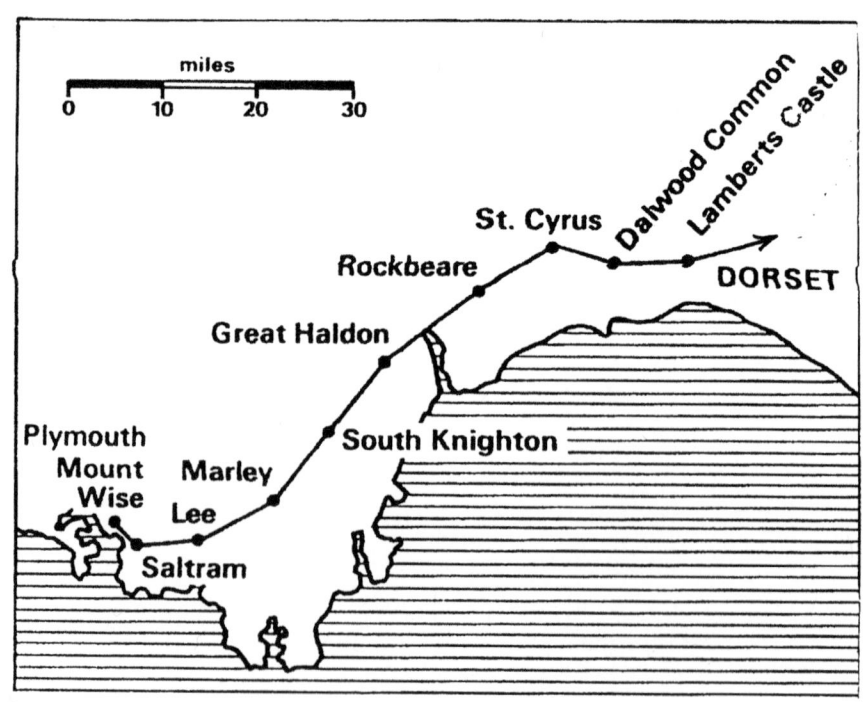

Map of the route.

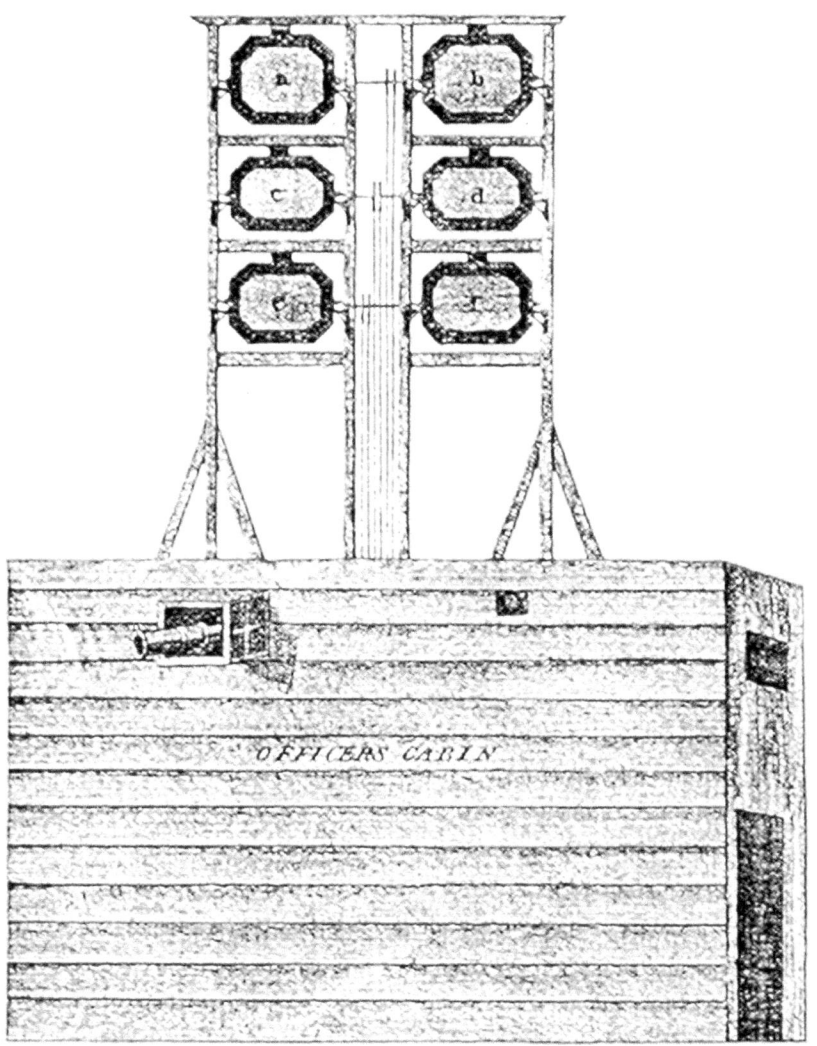

Plymouth onboard HMS *Imperieuse*; via the telegraph the Admiralty learned of his arrival and sent him an order to attend at Whitehall which he received within an hour of anchoring.'

DEVONSHIRE

45

Tollhouses

Many of the tollhouses throughout the country have reverted to private use, and Devon is no exception. Most are unremarkable, being utilitarian structures designed for a specific purpose, yet there are a few that are unusual or have unusual features, and they deserve a mention.

The most curious tollhouse and the only one of its type in the

Yealmbridge Hut.
(Peter Stanier)

Yealmbridge toll
board.

county, if not the whole country, is the little stone toll hut at Yealmbridge (SX593520), just east of the main tollhouse by the bridge (SX590520). Toll huts, such as this, were sited to catch travellers using side roads and it is not thought that they were constantly manned, probably only during daylight hours or on busy occasions. Both were owned by the Modbury Trust.

The smallest and oldest tollhouse in the county is operated by the Lyme Regis Trust at Newton Poppleford (SX079895). Built in 1758, it is a thatched, single-storey building with two bays, and is situated near the junction of the Exeter–Dorchester road (A3052) and the road to Budleigh Salterton (A376), and although now extended, it still retains its character.

A tollhouse belonging to the Honiton Trust, on the road to Dorchester (A35T) on the outskirts of Honiton, is unusual on several counts; its castellated bow front has tall pointed windows and doorway, and, more importantly, it has retained the ornamental iron gates which once closed the road, although in the interest of modern traffic flow, the road has been widened and the gates moved back so they no longer close the road. However, the origin of its extremely odd name – Copper Castle or Copper House (ST172005) – is unclear. The 'castle' bit is obvious, but does 'Copper' refer to the name of a family who lived there as toll keepers, or to the cost of passing through the gates – 'copper' being the old term for a penny or copper coinage?

Toll boards itemising the charges for vehicles, livestock and other road users can be seen in museums throughout the country, but Devon is fortunate in having one in situ in its original position at Yealmbridge (SX593520).

There were no uniform charges throughout the county, as each Turnpike Trust would set suitable charges for their area, just as they would exempt certain goods carried to boost the local economy in Devon, such as lime and sand which were both important for agriculture. The imposition of tolls on their local roads was greatly resented at first, but the improvements to the roads themselves were gradually accepted as the ease and speed of travel between towns, cities and the

The toll house at Newton Poppleford.

Copper Castle, Honiton, *c.* 1905.

Below: The 'Take Off' stone and hitching stone, Beardon.

capital became apparent, especially in the carrying of mail.

There is one other roadside curiosity that should be mentioned here. At Beardon (SX518842) there is a 'taking-off' stone which marked the point where a toll-free extra horse, which had helped haul a heavily laden wagon up the hill, had to be unhitched.

DEVONSHIRE

46

Guiding Lights

The provision of beacons, either as guides or as warnings, is as old as the Egyptians, with their 450ft-high lighthouse of Pharos at Alexandria. As early as the thirteenth century, the religious orders in this country had anchorites or hermits tending beacons around the coasts of Britain, such as those on The Island at St Ives in Cornwall and on St Aldhelm's Head near Worth Matravers in Dorset.

The little chapel of St Nicholas (SS524478) on Lantern Hill, a promontory sheltering the small harbour at Ilfracombe, was first recorded as showing a light for seamen in the fourteenth century, but whether this was a tallow candle in a window or a cresset (brazier) is not known. It was, however, of such importance that King Henry VIII gave 'indulgancies' to those penitents who helped to keep the light burning. The chapel is still there today, standing high above the town and harbour.

The notorious Eddystone Reef, some 12 miles off the coast of Plymouth, has a long history. In just one year during Queen Elizabeth I's reign, over fifty vessels foundered there. In 1696, a London merchant, Henry Winstanley, after losing his second ship on the Eddystone Rocks, decided that to prevent further loss to both himself and to others, he would build a lighthouse upon them. The result was a glorious octagonal wooden construction, with a glass lantern room in which candles were burnt to provide the light, but alas, on

Lantern Hill,
Ilfracombe.

27 November 1703, a terrible gale destroyed
the structure, and Winstanley, who was visiting
the lighthouse that night to make repairs, along
with five other occupants, all lost their lives. Its
importance had not been lost upon the Trinity
Brethren, and they at once built a replacement,
also from wood, which survived until 1759 when
the candles, catching the cupola alight 'flaming
like a great torch', burnt it down.

It was clear that a more solid structure was
needed and the great engineer, James Smeaton,
was consulted; he designed and built a lighthouse
that was to be the model for all those built in the
future. Its round, smooth and elegant shape could
withstand the onslaught of the highest waves, for
each block of stone from which it was constructed
was dovetailed into the next and made watertight
by the use of hydraulic cement from Watchet,
Somerset. The lantern was lit by twenty-four
tallow candles, giving a brilliant light. (It was
recorded that these candles cost 1*s* 6½*d* an hour to
burn.) This lighthouse survived until 1879 and would have survived
longer had not the rocks upon which it had been built decayed. The
present Eddystone Lighthouse was built some 100ft from the stump
of Smeaton's Tower. Such was the regard in which Smeaton was held

Smeaton's
lighthouse,
Plymouth Hoe
and Teignmouth
Beacon. *(Both:
Peter Stanier)*

that his tower was taken down, stone by stone,
and re-erected on Plymouth Hoe (SX478539) as a
lasting memorial to him, and to act as a beacon in
Plymouth Sound. It is now open to the public.

With the upsurge in trade for ball-clay and
granite from the Newton Abbot area at the
beginning of the nineteenth century, the small
port of Teignmouth became much busier; there
was, however, a spit of sand at the mouth of the
River Teign which was troublesome to navigate.
In 1845 the Harbour Board built a rather dinky
little lighthouse (SX940724) which stands at just
34ft high, and, although it looks like a lighthouse
with its cast-iron lantern, it was in fact a red
beacon light. Some of the sand spit has now been
reclaimed and the little light is now a feature of
the Den (as the gardens along the esplanade are
called).

As would be expected in a county which has
such dangerous coastlines, Devon has several

working lighthouses, all now automated. On the north coast they are situated at Foreland Point, Bull Point and Hartland Point, with two on Lundy Island; while on the south coast, they can be found at Berry Head and Start Point. There is nothing unusual about any of them – with the exception of Berry Head (SX946566). Berry Head is said to be 'the shortest yet the highest in the country', for although the lighthouse is only 16ft tall, it stands atop the 200ft-high cliffs of Berry Head, near Brixham, and its white light can be seen 14 miles out to sea. In lighthouses, the rotation of the lens was controlled by the descent of weights, as in a grandfather clock. Normally the wires on which the weights were suspended were in a tube within the lighthouse, but at Berry Head this was impossible; so a 140ft deep shaft was sunk beneath the lighthouse to accommodate the weights, which had to be regularly wound up by the lighthouse keeper. Today, all optics and lights are electric, although at first, when the lighthouse on Berry Head was built in 1906, it was operated by acetylene gas from its own plant.

DITTISHAM

47

Map Ref
SX671545

The Anchor Rock

Right in the middle of the navigable River Dart, near Dittisham, at its narrowest point between Dartmouth and Totnes, is the Anchor Rock. Covered at high tides, it was always a hazard to shipping, but even more so to a section of local and Dartmouth residents. Should the wives of seamen not heed their menfolk's wishes or become scolds, then they were taken to the Anchor Rock where they were left to cool their heels (and at high tide rather more than that) until they had learnt their lesson – a natural ducking stool!

Another story goes that Sir Walter Raleigh sat on Anchor Rock to smoke his silver pipe – perhaps he was banished there because of objections to the tobacco smoke permeating Greenway House, where he sometimes stayed.

DREWSTEIGNTON

The Last Castle

48

Map Ref
SX722900

Seen from afar, Castle Drogo, perched high above the wooded valley of the River Teign with views of Dartmoor, looks every inch a medieval castle guarding its Lord's demesne. On closer inspection, the building loses some of its defensive appearance and becomes instead a large country house with pretensions of grandeur. Built on a grand scale, it was designed by one of the country's greatest architects, Sir Edwin Lutyens, and was the last castle to be built in Britain.

Sir Julius Drewe made his fortune by selling tea grown on the family's Indian plantations directly to the public, thus cutting out the middleman. He built up a nationwide chain of grocery shops – the Home and Colonial Stores – and after only six years, took on retirement and the trappings of the landed gentry. It was an age for the newly rich to build themselves grand houses – Sir Henry Peek, of Peek Frean Biscuits fame, had erected his mansion at Rousdon near Seaton at the end of the nineteenth century.

Drewe was convinced that his family was descended from Drogo de Teigne, who came over with William the Conquerer and gave his name to Drewsteignton, so when 450 acres of Glebe lands came up for sale there in 1910, Julius bought them and immediately decided on both the site for his new ancestral home and the architect, with the building commencing in 1911. The war however interrupted proceedings, and the castle was not completed until 1930. Sadly, Julius only enjoyed Castle Drogo for a year, dying in 1931.

The castle is now owned by the National Trust and is well worth visiting, for the scenery is stunning, especially if one has walked up from Fingle Bridge; the architecture is typical Lutyens, rather heavy, but his little chapel inside the castle is magnificent.

DUNCHIDEOCK

Haldon Belvedere

Major-General Stringer Lawrence was the founder of the Indian Army of the East India Company and Sir Robert Palk (1717–98), a civil servant, was its Paymaster General, later to become Governor of Madras. Palk and Lawrence became great friends, and when Palk retired to Haldon House, Lawrence, a bachelor, was a frequent visitor; when he died in 1775, he left his considerable estate to Palk and his children, some £50,000. Lawrence was buried in St Michael and All Angels Church at Dunchideock and a plaque reads, 'The desperate state of affairs in India, becoming prosperous endeared him to his country'.

Haldon Belvedere.

Palk, however, wanted a more conspicuous memorial to his friend and in 1788 built Lawrence Castle, now better known as Haldon Belvedere, on the highest point of his Haldon estate. This is now the most prominent landmark in Devon, for it can be seen from Dartmoor, Exmoor, the Blackdown Hills and even, on a very clear day, from Portland in Dorset.

It is triangular in plan with round angle turrets; it is castellated and has Gothic pointed windows, with the ballroom on the first floor being used for parties by the Palks. In the entrance hall are panels (behind shutters) recording Lawrence's career and a larger-than-life Coade stone statue of him – after Scheermaker's depiction of him in the old India Office. He is dressed as a Roman general with one arm raised and a cloak sweeping to the ground – this was an additional feature put in to support the statue when it was being fired – and it is highly appropriate that the statue looks out over Exeter.

Statue of Stringer Lawrence made from Coade Stone.

Mrs Eleanor Coade (1733–1821) was one of Devon's most eminent, if little-known daughters. She was born in Exeter but lived and worked at Lambeth in London, where she had her studios and factory. Here she employed artists to mould statuary and building ornamentations; these were then cast in Coade stone; weather-resistant ceramic stoneware made to Eleanor's own secret formula, which were then fired in a kiln. The superb statuary and decorations which were produced by her factory were used by all the leading architects and builders of the day, from Sir John Soane to Robert Adam, and examples can be seen in most of the great houses of the period and throughout London.

Mrs Coade (the Mrs was an honorary title Eleanor gave herself to help her as a businesswoman), maintained her contact with the West Country, having a holiday home at Lyme Regis, left to her by an uncle. Although many church memorials are made of Coade stone, there are few examples of her statuary in Devon, the one in Haldon Belvedere being the finest.

Ninety-nine steps: the longest unsupported cantilevered staircase in the UK.

DUNKERSWELL

Wolford Chapel

50
Map Ref
ST137052

Along the road from Honiton to Dunkerswell are prominent signs, emblazoned with a maple leaf, directing visitors to Wolford Chapel. On following these signs, the visitor will eventually find themselves in a narrow, moss-grown lane, at the end of which is a rather small, unprepossessing church, beside which is a tall flagstaff flying the flag of the province of Ontario, Canada.

The fact is, the church was given to the province of Ontario in 1966 by the then owner of Wolford House, the publisher Sir Geoffrey Harmsworth. But why was it given and from a quick glance at the visitor's book in the church, why is it a place of pilgrimage for Canadians?

Wolford House was once the home of General John Graves Simcoe (1752–1806) and the little church was built by him in 1800. General Simcoe joined the army when he was eighteen, and during the American War of Independence, commanded the First American Regiment (Queen's Rangers). In 1791, he was appointed the first Lieutenant General of the newly-formed Province of Upper Canada, and during his energetic administration, he improved communications, encouraged immigration and founded the town of York, which later became Toronto. He went on to become Governor and Military Commander of St Domingo, commanded the Western Military Division when England was threatened by a French invasion between 1801 and 1804, and in 1806, was appointed Commander-in-Chief of India. However, he died before he could take up the post and was buried in this church, having bought the Wolford Estate in 1784.

Simcoe's wife, Elizabeth, and his five daughters (all unmarried), Eliza, Henrietta, Caroline, Sophie and Katherine, are all buried here. Another daughter, also Katherine, and a son, John Cornwall, died in infancy in Canada. His other son, Francis Gwillian, 'died in the breach at the siege of Badajoz [Spain], April 6th 1812 in the 21st year of his life'. Inside the church, over the pulpit, General Simcoe's life is aptly summed up: 'As for me and my house we will serve the Lord. XXIV 15 MDCCCII'. The chapel is administered by the John Graves Simcoe Memorial Foundation, Ontario.

On the walls of the church of St Nicholas in Dunkerswell are six corbels depicting the faces of General Simcoe's wife and five daughters (whose grandfather, incidentally, fell with Wolfe at the siege of Quebec in 1759). These were put up in their memory for the charity and kindness they showed to the poor and sick throughout the neighbourhood.

EAST BUDLEIGH

51
Map Ref
SY050851

Sir Walter Raleigh's Birthplace

When Walter Raleigh of Farwell near Cornwood, married Joan Drake of Exmouth, he purchased the large farmstead of Hayes Barton at East Budleigh so that his wife could remain near her family. It was also conveniently close to his manors at Withycombe Raleigh and Colaton Raleigh. It was here at Hayes Barton in 1552 that Joan gave birth to a son, who was to become the great Sir Walter Raleigh, scourge of the Spanish Main and favourite of Queen Elizabeth I. It is said that with his diamond ring he had etched on a window where he knew the Queen would see it the line 'Fain would I climb, yet fear I to fall', to which Elizabeth added underneath: 'If thy heart fail thee, climb not at all'.

Raleigh did fall – out of favour with the Queen – and was incarcerated in the Tower for treason before being beheaded. Raleigh's wife so loved him that she kept his embalmed head in a red leather bag for twenty-nine years until she died! Then his head was buried with his body.

While in prison Raleigh wrote his epic book *History of the World*, of which the poet James Thompson (1700–47) and author of 'Rule Britannia', thought so highly that he penned:

> In Raleigh mark, then, every glory mixed
> Whose breast with all
> The sage, the patriot, and the hero burned.
> His mind
> Explored the vast extent of ages past
> And with his prison hours enriched the world.

Hayes Barton.

The long, thatched farmhouse of Hayes Barton, with its gables and projecting porch, remains today much as it was in the sixteenth century, and although it is not open to the public, it can clearly be seen from Hayes Lane.

Raleigh's childhood at Budleigh is etched in most people's minds by the famous painting by Sir John Millais (1829–96), 'The Boyhood of Raleigh'. This shows the young Raleigh and a friend listening with rapt attention to some tale of the sea recounted by an old sea salt. The low wall by which they are sitting can still be seen in the charming town of Budleigh Salterton, where the promenade along the top of the pebble beach joins the town.

EXETER

The House that Moved

52
Map Ref
SX914922

Even though Exeter had been laid out by the Romans on a grid system, traffic flow in the 1950s had become a problem in the old city, and an inner relief by-pass road was planned. Hitler had cleared away many of the buildings along its proposed route but one stood resolutely in the way – 16 Edmund Street, a fifteenth-century timber-framed merchant's house. Conservationists were up in arms at the thought of its demolition, so the city council boldly decided to move it bodily to a new site, something that had never been attempted in this country previously.

Like many Tudor townhouses, each of its upper floors overhung those below, making it top heavy, and its original oak framing (some timbers were 13in square) also made it extremely heavy. The house's architectural features had to be retained, including the oak window

frames with their cusped trefoil headings, although the mud plasterwork infilling the timbers had to be taken out.

The whole building was first securely 'crated' with ten tons of oak timber framing; under this were placed small iron wheels which were to run on rails to the new site. This new site was at the bottom of Bartholomew Street, opposite St Mary Steps Church and facing up Stepcote Hill with its little cluster of similarly-aged buildings – a move of about 300ft up a steep incline of 1:10.

Early on the morning of 12 December 1961 the move was commenced with the aid of hydraulic jacks, inches at a time. This delicate move was made more difficult by the house in its framing, which had to be kept absolutely upright (owing to it being so top-heavy). A plumb line from the roof ensured it was kept stable. In spite of one snag – when the framing caught on a kerb – the move was completed in two days, and was attended by photographers, television cameras and film-makers – to say nothing of the hundreds of enthusiastic onlookers.

Today, after renovation and new mud plaster infilling of the timber framing, the house looks as though it had stood on its present site for all of its 600 years. The whole operation cost £8,000.

53

Map Ref
SX917927

EXETER

The Iron Bridge

It is not apparent nowadays why this North Street bridge was built, but in the days of horse traffic, the steep streets on both sides of the Longbrook valley caused great problems, especially as it was the main coaching road heading north out of Exeter. Because of existing houses, businesses and works along the streets, an embanked road across the valley was out of the question, so a bridge was proposed. The first suggestion was for a suspension bridge, but a cast-iron bridge was agreed upon by the Exeter Turnpike Trust and the city's improvements commissioners. It was opened to traffic in 1834.

Its 24ft-wide carriageway is 800ft long, with masonry causeways at each end and six cast-iron arches in the centre, each having a span of 40ft. The cast-iron sections were made at Russell & Brown's

Blaina Ironworks in South Wales, and were transported to Exeter by sea.

When the little Longbrook stream was eventually culverted (it had virtually become an open sewer), the last obvious reason for the construction of this fine example of nineteenth-century civil engineering disappeared, although the use for which it was built is still appreciated.

EXETER

54
Map Ref
SX914922

Matthew the Miller

During the medieval period, the most direct way into Exeter from the quayside, both for pedestrians and packhorses, was through the West Gate, then up the steep flight of steps known as Stepcote Hill, which led into the heart of the city. This was the route taken daily by Matthew, the miller at Cricklepit Mill, which was between the West Gate and the quays. Matthew was highly regarded for his probity and his punctuality, for it was said of his daily business visits to the city that 'one could set one's clock by him'.

After his death, he was commemorated by a single-hand clock, which consisted of a square stone dial below a niche in which the seated figure of Matthew, who nodded his head and struck the hours, was flanked by two jacks (possibly his sons) who struck the quarters. Made in 1619–21 by Exeter craftsman Matthew Hoppin, the clock was set high on the tower of the red sandstone church of St Mary Steps, at the bottom of West Street on the corner with Stepcote Hill. It was erected by two churchwardens who, fortunately for posterity, disagreed so violently as to who paid for what that they went to court, so leaving an official and contemporary record:

> Clock and Diall were made [for] and set up by the sd James Taylor [a churchwarden] . . . in the yeare 1619 and paid for by him . . . But he the sd Mathew Symonds [the other churchwarden] in the said yeare 1621 did only set up the two Jacks which play at every qr of an howre and another statue of tymbre called Matthew the Miller sitting in his chaire wch playeth out at every howers end, & also the two quarter bells under the feet of the sd two Jacks and the name of the sd Mathew Symonds in full letters & the yeare of our Lord (1621) guilded with gould, with a loader horse and baggs uppon him and a loader upon that carved in Free stone and the portrayture of the Mil house & of ye trees growing before the same likewise Carved in the same stone. . .

The clock mechanism was replaced in 1725 and the original Classical stone surround with the names, date and mill house was also replaced by the present ogee-headed canopy during the eighteenth century. The clock, with the symbols of the zodiac, had minutes added to the dial at the same time, but otherwise remains the same.

A rhyme told by an old lady in Taunton, who died in 1779 aged 101, went:

> Matthew the Miller's alive,
> Tho' Matthew the Miller's dead;
> Every hour, in Westgate Tower,
> Matthew the Miller nods his head.

Matthew still nods his head and kicks the hours and the two jacks strike the quarters in remembrance of his useful life. Perhaps they were put up as an object lesson for the local parishioners, for in the seventeenth century the parish was described as 'the most ignorant and profane part of the city'!

55

Map Ref
SX918926

EXETER

Parliament Street

Parliament Street is a 50m long alleyway which dates from the fourteenth century. It runs from just past the Guildhall in the High Street to Waterbeer Street, and is the narrowest street* in the world, its width varying from 25in to 45in. The alleyway is, in fact, too narrow for a large person to walk through in comfort and there is a story of a thief being chased by a policeman, who, on running through the alley, escaped because the officer was too stout to follow!

Until 1832 it was just a 'cut through' between the two streets called Small Lane; an insalubrious alley full of garbage and worse. However, in 1832, the great Parliamentary Reform Bill was eventually passed by the Whig government under Lord Grey, but not until the Tory majority in the House of Lords, who violently opposed it, had been threatened by the creation of enough Whig peers to see the bill through! It was then that the little alley was given the name Parliament Street – possibly in sardonic humour or to 'cock a snook' at the government! Anyway, it was given a cast-iron nameplate, and in 1959, the county council decided to place a brass plaque at the entrance in the High Street to celebrate its uniqueness which reads, 'Parliament Street – believed to be the narrowest street in the world. Width 25" increasing to 45"'.

---

* The dictionary definition of a street is a 'road in a town lined with houses, broader than a lane'.

EXETER

The Tunnels

56
Map Ref
SX923925

From the twelfth century, the walled city of Exeter, in spite of having many springs and wells, could not provide enough water to satisfy its growing population. There were strong springs to be found outside the city walls, but because Exeter was built on a low hill, water could not be brought to parts of the city in open runnels by gravity – as it could in the towns of Tiverton and Honiton.

The problem was overcome by cutting tunnels and passageways through the hill so that lead pipes laid in them could carry water (by gravity) to the public conduits. The walls and roofs of some were made from the natural rock through which they had been cut, while others had to be lined with stone; they varied in height from 3ft 4½in to 14ft 9in and from 1ft 7in to 3ft wide. The lead pipes could not be buried as are water mains today, because they were made of sheets of lead, curved to meet at the top, the joining edges sealed by heating. Constant leaks occurred; hence the need for tunnels to get at them.

Over the past 200 years, after they became redundant, some leats have been damaged by building work, trenching for modern services and even deliberately by thieves breaking into them for the lead.

Enough survive though, for a labyrinth of tunnels to remain under the city's streets, ancient buildings and new developments; some of these – the earliest dating from 1245 – are open to the public, and can be reached by steps in Eastgate Street. Contact the Royal Albert Memorial Museum & Art Gallery for times and charges: (01392) 665858.

EXMOUTH

Point-in-View

57
Map Ref
SY009834

In 1796 two cousins, Jane and Mary Parmiter, built an unusual house, the sixteen-sided 'A La Ronde' on the hill behind Exmouth, overlooking both the town and wide sweep of Torbay. They also formed the famous shell gallery within the house, which is now a popular visitor attraction in the property owned by the National Trust. Just up the lane, however, is an even more curious group of buildings, also built by the two cousins in 1811, called Point-in-View.

In the middle of an open field, surrounded by a low wall, 'sits' a low building, comprising a chapel with a dumpy spire, in its centre, and once surrounded by four almshouses for single women. The chapel was, and still is, Primitive Methodist, and its chaplain had two rooms at the front, and adjoining those, a small schoolroom dedicated to

Point-in-View
from the west.

teaching six local farm girls. A schoolteacher was allocated her own one-roomed quarters, and the girls were provided with a new outfit of clothes every year, together with a new bonnet.

In about 1830 the chaplain (perhaps now having a wife), decided that his quarters were too small and he was provided with a two-storied manse a little to the east. His old rooms were then incorporated into the chapel, which besides increasing its size also allowed in far more light; previously the only light which came into the chapel was from four little windows set in the spire. The schoolroom is still as it was, a wooden desk (and two inkwells) and a girl's bonnet in a glass case. In the 1960s, the almshouses were amalgamated into one and three modern bungalows were built near the manse. Regular services are still taken by the chaplain and the chapel is frequently used for weddings. There is now a paved path but any vehicles have to go over the field!

In 1830, Mary Parmiter made Point-in-View a charity, and so it remains today.

58

Map Ref
SS403243

FAIRY CROSS

Bus Stop

The name Fairy Cross conjures up a vision of a quaint and picturesque hamlet, whereas in fact, the village consists of a dull collection of houses straggling the busy A39 – the so-called Atlantic Highway from Bideford to Bude. On the other hand, the words 'utilitarian' and 'functional' are those usually applied to bus shelters, but not this one at

Fairy Cross, for which one has to stop to make sure it isn't a holy well or wayside shrine somehow missed on a previous journey.

Constructed in 2006 as a gift to the village from Michael Connor, of the Portledge Estate, it was built to commemorate Bob Davies, who was the manager of their Cockington Farm for twenty-five years.

It is six-sided and built of stone, with carved granite window openings and a doorway, under a 'witch's hat' slated roof. Its floor is tiled, with a compass rose in the centre, while on the outside are two slabs of slate with the words 'Fairy Cross' cut onto them and then gilded. To cap it all there is a weather-vane in the shape of a winged fairy!

This is a truly delightful work of modern architecture which will no doubt become a listed building in the future.

FILLEIGH

Sham Castle

59

Map Ref
SS672286

After Lord Clinton, the first Baron Fortescue, had built his new Palladian mansion during the 1730s, he wanted something eye-catching on the hill behind it. The result was the 'sham castle', which was so effective that his mansion took its name from it – Castle Hill.

From a distance the sham castle, with its turrets and castellations, really does look like a castle from a storybook, but the nearer one gets to it the clearer it appears be what actually it is – a folly; an empty shell having no practical use, not even as a prospect tower. One would never have been needed, for the Fortescue estate can be seen from the ground; west, south and east, as far as the eye can see, and the north would have been the same before the woods grew up and largely hiding the new A361(T) road.

The landscaped gardens of Castle Hill appear to continue right up the hill to the castle, but even that is a sham, for the steep, grassy slope is not part of the gardens but an ordinary pasture field; however, in place of hedges or fences, it is surrounded by that well-loved eighteenth-century feature – a ha-ha.

During the summer months, Castle Hill grounds are open to the public and the climb up to the castle is worth the effort.

60 FLETE

Map Ref
SX 630513

Bob Bunker's Tree

The level parkland, bounded by the River Erme and a small tributary, is overlooked by the grand Flete House, largely rebuilt in the 1870s, sitting as it does on a lofty eminence. Like all parkland, it is dotted with trees, many of them planted at the end of the eighteenth century under the supervision of the Bulteel family's steward, Bob Bunker, who died in around 1845 and is buried in Yelverton churchyard.

Bob Bunker's tree.

John Crocker Bulteel thought greatly of him and had a memorial to him erected beneath a large sycamore; it is a 4ft high, 1ft square granite column surmounted by an orb, and with a brass plate on which a poem is inscribed as beautifully as a memorial in any church in the country:

The stone and tablet beside Bob Bunker's tree.

We Christen thee
Bob Bunker's Tree
For we have bound thee round
With gentle waters fresh and new
Sparkling like the morning dew
Upon thy verdant mound.
Grow, Grow,
For thou art young
Not yet three score
Grow on ye Sycamore.
Grow, grow, Robin, grow
Thy pretty namesake many a day
Shall lurk beneath each sheltering bough
And O'er thy waters play.
Robin grow
Well-a-day . . .
The man that hauls thee down. 1845

The reason for the reference to Robin is unknown. It could have been Bob's Christian name, but the truth is we shall never know. Sadly, the memorial is not accessible to the public.

HACCOMBE

61
Map Ref
SX897701

The Horseshoes

The parish of Haccombe with the thirteenth-century church of St Blaize as its hub, has never been anything but a few scattered farms and houses, the majority of which, until comparatively recently, would have belonged to the Carew family, whose home, Haccombe House, is St Blaize's closest neighbour. It is therefore only to be expected that the church holds many of the Carew tombs and brasses.

During the fourteenth century, St Blaize became a collegiate church with an archpriest at it head, and although the college closed a century or so later, the title of archpriest has survived to this day and through custom, declines to answer the citation when visited by a bishop or archdeacon. In 1913, the parish was joined to that of its neighbour, Coffinswell, but the joint incumbent answers the citation for Coffinswell only. Until 1982 St Blaize had no churchwardens and the archpriest continues to wear lawn sleeves like a bishop, and a fur stole or amyss. Stranger still is what can be seen on the south door of the church.

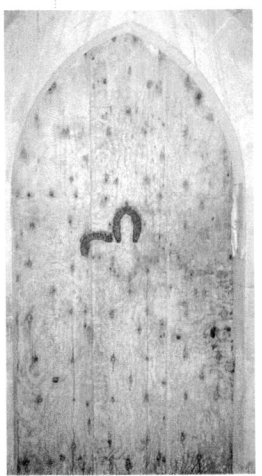

The church door.

In 1627 the current head of the Carew family had a dispute with Sir Arthur Campernowne of Dartington and Lord of Totnes, as to whose horse was the best – Campernowne's Barbary courser or Carew's Devonshire roan. To settle the matter each wagered his manor on which horse could swim farthest out to sea. They went to Torre Abbey beach and rode into the sea. Campernowne's horse tired first (there is no account of how far they swam but it was said halfway across to Brixham), and so tired had the Barbary become that Carew's roan had to bring them all back safely to shore. So Carew got the Manor of Dartington, and in thanks for this and to his horse's strength, he had its four horseshoes nailed to St Blaize's south door. One still hangs there, together with half of another and the nail marks of the other two.

Although the church is usually kept locked, it is worth the short drive up to Haccombe from the main Milber to Stokeinteignhead road if only to view some of the most glorious countryside in Devon.

HALBERTON

62
Map Ref
ST005127

The 'Sand' Spring

On turning off the main road through the village to Lower Town, the street dips down to an embanked road with a large millpond on its northern side. It is said that this pond never freezes and that in winter steam rises from the surface!

'Eruptions' of sand about 3ft below water surface.

The water feeding this pond comes from a powerful spring at its extreme northern end, welling up from an aquifer estimated to be 120ft below the surface. Coming from that depth, the water maintains a constant temperature of around 10°C – warm enough to prevent the pond from freezing, and forming a mist on the surface of the pond in the cold winter air.

The spring itself is about 15ft across and 3ft deep, with the 'active' area measuring roughly 6ft in diameter. This area is sometimes referred to as the 'Sand Spring'. Across the surface of this active area occur small, volcano-like eruptions of fine sand (which contain minute particles of a carboniferous nature), brought up by the spring water; these form, subside and reform in a constantly changing pattern. The sand well is extremely deep, for it was plumbed some years ago and at 50ft, the bottom had not yet been reached. Not a safe place for paddling, but fortunately this part of the pond is on private property.

HALLSANDS

A Vanished Village

63
Map Ref
SX817388

At the end of the nineteenth century, Hallsands was a tiny fishing village with twenty or so small boats engaged in crabbing or when the shoals of mackerel came in, seine netting. The village was built along a ledge of rock with a low seawall protecting over thirty houses and a pub – the London Inn. It was sheltered to the south by Start Point and to the east and north by a large shoal of shingle offshore and a steep shingle beach, rising almost to the level of the village's one street. The high tide came up to about 30yds from the seawall, leaving an ample beach on which to draw up the boats.

In 1897 the Admiralty planned an extension to the dockyard at Devonport, and needing vast amounts of sand and shingle the contractors, were authorised to dredge from the shoal offshore from Hallsands. In spite of protests from the fishermen and warnings that the removal of shingle would lower the level of the beach, thus threatening their homes, 650,000 tons of material was dredged up until it was stopped in 1901, but by this time it was too late.

The beach below the village was now 7ft lower and the high tides were reaching up to 10yds from the seawall. In 1903, the wall was breached; most of the London Inn collapsed, four houses were made uninhabitable, and the new boat slip was partially demolished as was a section of the main street. Although remedial action was undertaken, with the seawall underpinned with concrete, the winter storms of 1917, coming in from the east, ensured the demise of the village.

By midnight on 26 January, four houses had been destroyed by waves; and with the following high tide on the 27th, the remaining houses collapsed one by one, their foundations being undermined by the retreating waves, and only one house was left standing by the end of the day. Twenty-nine houses and most of their contents were lost, although fortunately, there was no loss of life; in all thirty-seven houses were destroyed by the sea – the entire village – with just one house surviving on the road leading down to the village. This house remained occupied by a very stubborn old lady (and her chickens) until her death in 1964.

After long, drawn out and litigious negotiations, the villagers obtained some compensation from the Admiralty, the government and the contractor who removed the shingle. Sixteen new homes were built above the old village, well back from the cliff edge, although many people left the village to live elsewhere. All that remains of the original village of Hallsands are a few broken walls and the shingle beach, many feet below where the seawall once stood.

Hallsands village, *c.* 1948.

64
Map Ref
SS221245

HARTLAND

The Quay

Even as late as the beginning of the nineteenth century the carriage of goods by road (given the state most were in) was a difficult undertaking, and whenever possible, these were transported by sea. Where there were no harbour facilities, the small coastal trading boats were beached at high tide, their cargos unloaded onto carts or packhorses at low tide, then re-floated when the tide came in. One of the wildest, rockiest and most dangerous stretches of coast is that due south of Hartland Point, which faces the full might of the Atlantic; there were beaches but they would have been extremely hazardous for 'beaching' vessels and, anyway, they were inaccessible.

The slipway to the beach. The stump of the old harbour wall can be seen in the centre. *(Author's Collection)*

It was therefore a measure of the need of those living in the Hartland village area for goods to be brought in by sea, that Warren Beach was made useable. South of the beach the cliffs were less sheer and in the sixteenth century, a track was made leading down to a small and level 'meadow' where an inn and storage facilities were built. Warren Beach was, to a certain extent, sheltered from the south by a large stack, Life Rock, and in the shelter of this, a quay was built. As can be seen in a very early photograph, the stone quay jutted out to the west, turning north then east to form a protective arm where boats could be beached in safety, with the goods being brought up via a cobbled slipway. Because it was so exposed to the waves frequent repairs had to be made; with road traffic increasing in the nineteenth century and the coming of the railway to Bideford in 1855, the quay lost its importance and repairs failed to be maintained. It sustained great damage during a storm in 1887, and in 1896, a further storm saw its demolition.

Today, only the slipway and the stump of the quay survive, although the inn does a flourishing trade in the summer months, for the track leading down to it is now a toll road. Warren Beach is not a safe beach for bathing but is used by hardier surfers, and even they must take heed of the old saying:

From Padstow Point to Hartland Light
Is a watery grave by day or by night.

HAYTOR

The Granite Railway

65
Map Ref
SX152778–
SX848747

To facilitate the transport of clay from his pits in the Teign Valley down the River Teign to the harbour at Teignmouth, James Templar, of Stover House, built a canal in 1790 – the Stover Canal – from Whitelake Channel on the River Teign up to its terminus at Ventiford. George Templar had, by then commenced quarrying for granite at Holwell Tor, and when contracts were obtained to supply building stone for many projects in London, including London Bridge, it was decided to build a horse tramway to bring the stone down to Ventiford.

'Points' near Haytor.

Horse tramways using iron rails were commonplace at the beginning of the nineteenth century, for by then there were over 3,500 miles of them in the country. They did, however, suffer from excessive wear, and the cost of bringing iron rails from South Wales around the coast to Teignmouth was great; but there was no need to use iron as granite would serve just as well and was far cheaper. Blocks of granite were cut 1ft 3in wide and 1ft thick, with outside flanges 3in deep and 7½in in width. These were of varying lengths and as their very weight made them extremely stable, there was no need to either tie them to each other or to have cross ties to the other rail, which were laid to a gauge of 4ft 3in between the flanges.

Horses were employed to draw the twelve-wheeled carts up from Holwell Quarries to Haytor, but thereafter, gravity took them down to Ventiford, with long poles used for braking. Horses drew the empty carts back. The distance to Ventiford was approximately 7 miles and fell over 1,200ft, so the actual length of the track was much greater, for there had to be many long curves to make the gradient easier and safer. There were many spurs to other quarries in the area around Haytor, and where they joined the main 'railway', the blocks were cut to make 'points'.

The 'railway' was opened in 1820 and finally closed in 1857, but the line can still be traced as far as Brimley, with a few of the granite milestones surviving. The stone rails and points are particularly easy to see and make for a pleasant walk in the area around Haytor.

HEMYOCK

A Pillory

Many Devon towns and villages have retained and cherished their old stocks, that effective way of punishing drunks and petty wrongdoers; some have even been given a little roof such as the one in the churchyard at Ottery St Mary.

The pillory was a much harsher form of punishment, for the miscreants had to stand for long periods with their head and hands held in an awkward and painful position; furthermore, they were unable to protect themselves from any form of physical abuse onlookers thought fit for the offence that they had committed. One of the only known surviving pillories in Devon is in the grounds of Hemyock Castle; not a real castle but on old fortified house.

In 1381, William Asthorp was given permission to fortify his Manor House, which he surrounded by an 18ft-high curtain wall, 5ft thick and with eight towers some 40ft high. There was a gatehouse and portcullis with a drawbridge over the moat which surrounded it, fed by the stream which now flows between the house and St Mary's Church. When the Civil War started, it was owned by the Pophams, a staunch Parliamentary family, and was used as a prison for Royalists. In 1643 it was besieged by the Royalists who captured the house and released the 200 prisoners. On the restoration of the monarchy in 1660, King Charles II ordered the castle to be slighted. As a result of this slighting, only fragments of the curtain wall and two towers remain, although the gatehouse is in a good state of preservation. This can be seen from the path which runs beside the stream, although the house itself is privately owned.

HONITON

The Glove is Up

67
Map Ref
ST163006

Traditionally, Honiton's Charter Fair commenced on the eve of the feast day of St Margaret, but it was later changed to the first Tuesday after 19 July, continuing until the following Saturday.

When a monarch granted a charter to a town to hold a fair, one of the orders stated 'That no man shall be arrested for any offence, save that of debt, for the duration of the Fair'. The start of the fair in Honiton is signified by the raising of a white glove on top of a pole, garlanded with flowers: this is carried by the Town Crier and paraded through the borough, after which it is placed prominently on the front of the old King's Arms Hotel, where it stays until Saturday, when it is transferred to the White Lion Inn at the far end of the High Street.

On the Tuesday, while the glove is being placed on the King Arms, a shovelful of hot pennies is thrown into the crowd – in days gone by they were nearly red hot, and there must have been great merriment with much blowing on burnt fingers!

'The Glove is Up' probably extended to minor misdemeanours, such as drunkenness, etc. More serious offenders would have been arrested as soon as the glove came down – if they were still around!

This custom of hoisting up a white glove is also carried out at Totnes and at Modbury, but the ceremonies there are not as elaborate as those witnessed at Honiton.

ILFRACOMBE

The Tunnels Beaches

68
Map Ref
SS516479

Like most towns and villages around the coast of Devon at the beginning of the nineteenth century, Ilfracombe wanted to cash in on sea bathing, made popular by King George III. It had a small harbour and a few rocky beaches, but nowhere visitors could bathe in comfort or safety. The two small secluded coves very near the town were inaccessible due to the steep cliffs.

In 1823, miners were brought over from South Wales to dig tunnels from the town to these beaches. The first and longest tunnel led directly to one cove, and another from there through a cliff spur, to the second cove. To make it possible for bathers to take a dip or swim in safety, each cove had a large sea-washed pool constructed, enclosed by concrete walls between the larger rocks; there were bathing machines on the beaches and rowing skiffs for the pools. Like

The Tunnel
Beaches Bath
House, 2007.

Below: Entrance
to the tunnels.

the present ponds on Hampstead Heath in London, one cove was reserved for ladies only and the other for gentlemen and boys. There was an entrance fee of 2*d* which helped pay for a man with a bugle to warn off any man who dared approach the ladies beach!

Another attraction was provided for the visitors at the entrance to the tunnels – hot and cold seawater baths – with wood burning boilers, both to heat the water and to pump it up from the nearest cove.

The Bath House is still there, although no longer fulfilling its original function; the tunnels and beaches remain a great attraction, although the wall forming the first pool (the gentlemen's) was destroyed during a gale in the 1960s. The other is well patronised, especially by children, for at low tide it makes a safe bathing and paddling area.

KINGSBRIDGE

69
Map Ref
SX732443

The Town Clock

The steep main street of Kingsbridge has some fine and interesting architecture; the wooden arcade of the market (the Shambles), old slate-hung houses and the early nineteenth-century Town Hall, with its rather Russian-looking clock crowning the roof. It is a large clock but only

The clock's blank
west face.

has three faces, for the one facing west is blank. There were streets, houses and also the churchyard on that side, so why no clock face?

The reason was due to the workhouse: the town council, in their wisdom, decided that could the inmates see the time, they would become clock watchers and their work would suffer, so the clock was given a blank face on that side!

KINGSWEAR

A Daymark

70
Map Ref
SX903503

High above Froward Point, east of the mouth of the River Dart, this curious 80ft-high structure was erected in 1864 by the Dartmouth

Harbour Commissioners as a 'daymark' to aid navigation. Standing on eight arched legs, it is hollow but with no steps up to the top. It was built on land belonging to Brownstone Farm, which was owned by Mr Seale-Hayne, a Member of the Commission. Although this looks as though it ought to have a light on its top, it was not built as a lighthouse but solely as a 'daymark' for visual use during the daylight hours; which is why so many church towers near the coast and visable from the sea, were painted white to act as 'daymarks'.

In Cornwall, on Gribbin Head near Fowey, there is another purpose-built 'daymark' but this one is solid and painted with coloured bands. All 'daymarks' were shown on Admiralty charts, including church towers used as such.

LUPPITT

The 'Harbour'

71
Map Ref
ST173064

During the latter half of the nineteenth century and the beginning of the twentieth, Luppitt had two football teams – the 'Sailors' and the 'Dockers' – the members of the respective teams living on either side of the little River Love, which divided the village. Until quite recently, where this brook crossed the road leading up to the church, there was a very wide, shallow ford. This was known as Luppitt Harbour (and is still known as such), with the male resident of the cottage directly east of the ford having the honorary title of harbourmaster! The last harbourmaster, Tim Davey, who died in 1982, had a postcard of 1905, coloured in the style of that era, depicting this wide ford, but with a much-reduced photograph of a battleship superimposed on the water!

Surprisingly, this phoney postcard has a basis in fact and makes a fascinating example of how folk stories come into being.

During the Civil War of 1642–6 between the Royalists under Charles I and the Parliamentarians under Cromwell, the Parliamentarians had a small army camped on Hartridge, an area of high, level ground to the east of Luppitt. The Royalists in the area were heavily outnumbered and called for reinforcements from their nearest garrison at Exeter. No soldiers could be spared but a small contingent of sailors was dispatched from Topsham. The story has it that they sailed up the brook from Budleigh Salterton, and on arrival scaled the steep, wooded slope of the hill, which to this day is named Luppitt Shore, and helped win the day for the Royalists.

LUPPITT

72

Map Ref
ST168067

The Pagan Font

The Norman font in the little church of St Mary's, Luppitt, is more worthy of note than the beautiful wagon-roof or the impressive gargoyles on the outside of the north wall. The font is square and the carvings on its four sides are barbaric in their representation. Nikolaus Pevsner describes them as 'centaur fighting two dragons, two men fighting each other with nail-shaped big clubs, a group of dachshund-like animals and a tree with dishevelled foliage'. (Could this be the tree of life treated by an exceptionally unconventional carver?) Another description says 'curious grotesques and a pagan centaur (note especially the priapus, which at first sight might be taken for a tail). It is possible that the image of the demon swallowing the top of the human head is a symbolic representation of demonic possession, the idea being that the demon is in charge of the thinking of the human being that it is attacking'. All writers, however, attest the pagan origins of the carvings and the assimilation of the old beliefs into the Christian religion.

In Greek mythology, Priapus was the son of Dionysus and Aphrodite, the god of reproductive power and fertility and the protector of shepherds, fishermen and farmers. He was later regarded as the chief deity of lasciviousness and obscenity, with the phallus as his attribute. It is no wonder that at some distant period, the font was taken from the church and tipped over the bank of a neighbouring field and was only found in the nineteenth century and restored to its rightful place in the church.

The carvings on three sides of the font – note the priapus.

According to one authority, the name Luppitt stems from 'Love-pit', after a religious order that once lived in the valley beside the little River Love, but was disbanded some time before the thirteenth century by the Lords of the Manor, the Mahuns of Ottery Mahun.

LYDFORD

The Prison

73
Map Ref
SX507848

At the time of the Domesday Survey in 1086, the small hamlet of Lydford was the fifth largest 'burg' in Devonshire, after Exeter, Tavistock, Barnstaple and Okehampton. The Normans built defensive earth ramparts on the spur of land between the gorge and another steep valley, and then in 1195, a more substantial square stone castle, not for defence but as a courthouse and prison to uphold the harsh Forest Laws. During the reign of King Edward I (1272–1307), the top two storeys became unsafe and were pulled down, the rubble completely filling the ground floor, with two new floors being built on the foundations of the old first floor. A ditch was dug around it with the earth being piled up against the ground floor wall, covering the windows and so giving it the appearance of a motte. One 12ft × 12ft area of the old ground floor was retained as a windowless prison – a sort of oubliette, which was thought of at the time 'as one of the most hideous, contagious and detestable places in the realm'.

The tinners in Devon, having separated from their opposite numbers in Cornwall during the fourteenth century, had their own stannary court or parliament which met in the open on Crockern Tor (SX614755) to fix their laws concerning the mining of tin. Lydford

was not a stannary town – where tin that had been mined and melted down was assayed and stamped – but because it had a readymade court and prison, this was taken over as the stannary prison, where anyone who broke the stannary laws would be incarcerated, often for months, before being tried. The prison had a terrible reputation, and as late as 1644, the Tavistock poet, William Browne, author of *Britannia's Pastorals*, wrote a long poem about it, the first lines being:

> I oft have heard of Lydford law
> How in the morn they hang and draw
> And sit in Judgement after. . .

How much of the prison's reputation came from the stannary laws or from the earlier Forest Laws, time has forgotten. It wasn't until 1512, however, when a Member of Parliament, Richard Strode, was put in prison for three weeks after he questioned the stannary court's laws, that the government curtailed their right to be above the national laws.

Even before the stannary court ceased to function in the late eighteenth century, the warden and his court must have found that sitting on Crockern Tor was rather too draughty and cold for their deliberations, and they repaired to the local hostelry, with the old stone table and chair on the tor being broken up for building stone.

The castle is now in the care of English Heritage and is freely accessible, and although it is roofless and an empty shell, it can nevertheless still be seen how superbly it had been built with phenomenally true walls.

LYDFORD

The Gorge

74
Map Ref
SX475833–
SX512846

Over the centuries since the last ice age, as the River Lyd came coursing down from the moors, it cut a deep, two-mile long channel for itself – Lydford Gorge. From the top of this sometimes precipitous ravine, its sides now clothed with trees, bushes and ferns, the only evidence of the little river is the sound as it leaps and tumbles over its boulder-strewn bed and the occasional glimpse of a swirling pool, the largest of which is the allegedly haunted Kitts Steps, so-called after an old woman who was said to have drowned there.

Lydford Gorge is a magical place to walk through, especially in the summer when much of it is enveloped in a dappled green light, but it is in no way spectacular. That is left to a small tributary stream coming off Henscott Moor as it falls over the edge of the gorge in a magnificent 100ft leap into the River Lyd below – a waterfall known as the White Lady (SX500835).

Legends abound throughout the world telling of water sprites, water nymphs or white ladies, as they are sometimes called, who materialise out of the sparkling spray and rainbows caused by cascading waters – perhaps the name of this waterfall stems from those distant sources.

The White Lady.

However, Lydford Gorge has a darker history, for it was home to a notorious band of outlaws and brigands – the Gubbins. The Revd Fuller, writing in 1661, recounts how, early in the fifteenth century, 'two strumpets being with child, fled hither to hide themselves, to whom certain lewd fellows resorted'. So this tribe of outlaws began and '. . . they lived in cotts (rather holes than houses) holding all in common, offend one offend all . . . they multiplied without marriage into many hundreds'. They supported themselves by sheep-stealing and brigandry, and were so fleet of foot on the moors that mounted soldiery sent to apprehend them could not catch them! It was not until the seventeenth century that they adopted a more Christian way of life, and to this day in Devon, something filthy is called 'gubbins'. When R.D. Blackmore came to write *Lorna Doone*, he based his protagonist's wild outlaw family, the Doones, living on Exmoor, on the Gubbins, even though they had long gone.

Most of Lydford Gorge is now owned by the National Trust, and for a fee one may walk the paths, walkways and little bridges along most of its length; but beware, for it can be extremely slippery.

75
Map Ref
SX988840

LYMPSTONE

Lympstone's little Big Ben

Once a small fishing village situated a little way up from the mouth of the River Exe, Lympstone, like Cockwood on the opposite bank of the wide estuary, used to harvest the plentiful shellfish of the river. Although illustrations of women cockle pickers are quite picturesque, in reality, it was a hard life and money must have been short. Charity was a feature of life in the late Victorian era and for a village such as Lympstone, it must have been a lifeline for many families.

Close to the tiny harbour, and almost on the village hard, stands a tall, brick-built clock tower, with crenulations around the top and the whole surmounted by a short spire; somewhat like a smaller version of St Stephen's Tower at the Palace of Westminster, often referred to as Big Ben. The inscription on this tower reads, 'This CLOCK-TOWER was erected in 1885 by W.H. PETERS ESQ. of Harefield in Memory of his wife MARY JANE to commemorate her kindness and sympathy for the poor of LYMPSTONE'.

In front of the clock tower, giving the area a comfortable, lived-in feel, are washing lines – now rarely seen in such a prominent position. What makes these exceptional is that the lines (still a jealously guarded right of those living in nearby houses) are strung on pulleys on high poles, the further ones being well below the high tide line, with the washing drying over the water and catching the breeze coming up the river.

Below: The clock tower and its attendant washing lines.

Below, right: An Exe Cockler, *c.* 1900.

LYNMOUTH

The Cliff Railway

This is Britain's shortest and steepest railway, and double-tracked at that! It is 862ft long, rises 500ft with a gradient of 1:1½, has a track width of 3ft 9in and, except for a slight rumble of wheels, is utterly silent – for there is no motor power, gravity doing all the work (although there are brakes!)

Two cars, on separate lines, are both connected to a steel cable, with each having a water ballast tank holding 24 tons of water. If the total weight of the bottom car (each can hold forty passengers) wishing to ascend exceeds that of the car waiting to come down, the driver discharges some water, making the top car slightly heavier, whereupon one car goes smoothly up and the other down, passing each other in the middle where the lines diverge slightly. When it reaches the top the ballast tank is refilled, ready for the next cycle, the water being supplied through a pipe from the West Lyn River, several miles away.*

The line was financed by Sir George Newnes, the publisher, who lived in Lynton, and was designed and built by a local builder, Bob Jones, in 1885.

The road up to Lynton has a gradient of 1:5 with acute hairpin bends, and even today, is not an easy drive, so getting building materials up to Lynton by horse and cart was extremely difficult. The flatbed wagons that Jones designed could take everything up, and the detachable cars were a good visitor attraction when opened in 1890. Besides the enjoyment it gives to the thousands of visitors who use it each year, it is also regularly used by locals to go shopping in Lynton.

Above: Going up.

Below: The limekilns.

In the early days of motoring, when cars couldn't cope with the steep hill, they were taken up on the flatbed for 7*s* 6*d*, and after the destruction caused by the disastrous floods of 1952, stranded cars were taken up once again. The railway closes for three months after Christmas.

The white, arched structure next to the bottom station is three, long-disused limekilns, where the limestone and culm, brought over from South Wales, was burnt to provide lime for agriculture and building.

---

* The hydraulic buffers that Jones invented for use at the bottom of the incline are now in use throughout the world.

77
Map Ref
SS705497

LYNTON

Valley of the Rocks

The valley of the Rocks, or Dane's Combe, is sited just west of Lynton, forming a small, wild arena, with rough grazing, heather and scattered boulders to the south, and ragged cliffs of rock to the north, which plunge down to the sea on their other side; all dominated by the towering Castle Rock. Although unseen, the sea can be heard crashing against the rocks below, and it is not difficult to imagine it as the setting for the cave of Mother Meldrum, the witch to whom Jan Ridd came for advice in R.D. Blackmore's *Lorna Doone*. The valley had now been somewhat tamed by its level bottom becoming a playing field and car park.

Long ago, herds of wild goats were a vital part of rural economy, especially in the north, providing meat, hides, hair, horn and hoof. The last wild herd roamed the Cheviot Hills in Northumberland, and when these were in danger of being wiped out in the nineteenth century, the owner of Lee Abbey (now a private house) rescued a few and brought them to a wild part of his estate – the Valley of Rocks – unintentionally making them an additional attraction to visitors; for when seen standing on the high rocks, they become smaller versions of Sir Edwin Landseer's 'Monarch of the Glen'.

Below: The Valley of Rocks, *c.* 1910.

Bottom: Castle Rock, Lee Tower and Jenny's Leap. (Devon, V.C. Clinton-Baddeley)

The area suited them and they thrived, to such an extent that they started to make nuisances of themselves by plundering farm crops and neighbouring gardens. This led to cries for them to be banished elsewhere, but a compromise was reached and they are now periodically culled, by shooting them with anaesthetising darts, before being removed to areas where undergrowth has to be controlled – the bird sanctuary at Mimsmere in Suffolk, is an example.

Situated just west of Dane's Combe is Lee Abbey, the sixteenth-century home of the de Wychalse family. Edward de Wychalse's daughter, Jenny, was seduced by a nobleman in the court of James I who, after she became 'with child', deserted her. In despair, she mounted her favourite white horse, rode to Duty Point and leapt into the sea. Duty Point has ever after been known as Jenny's Leap (SS594496).

MAMHEAD

The Castle

Robert Newman was a businessman from Dartmouth whose family made their money from the fishing industry and from importing wines from Portugal.

Newman purchased the Mamhead estate in the 1820s, and had the old house demolished and in its place a new house designed by Anthony Salvin in the Grand Gothic fashion. Salvin made his name as an architect with Mamhead House and went on to build houses in this style throughout the country. Newman also required stables, coach houses, a laundry and a brewery, and had Salvin design suitable premises for them – probably the most unusual building for these purposes anywhere in the world.

Above: The gatehouse and fake portcullis.
Below: A bartizan tower complete with clock!

There had been an ancient medieval castle on the hill immediately above the house and for this site Salvin designed the stables and outbuildings as a castle based on the one at Belsay in Northumberland. It was built from the local, reddish stone with two square guard towers beside the arched entrance with its fake portcullis, and with round bartizan corner towers. (Bartizan towers have projecting battlements with holes through which boiling oil, etc. could be poured onto the attackers beneath). The walls tower over the house and gardens (laid out in the previous century by Capability Brown), although there were more modern touches, such as the windows and a clock on one of the towers.

Newman later became MP for Exeter and eventually became Lord Newman of Mamhead. The Castle no longer serves its original purposes but has become a suite of business offices. It is not accessible to the public.

79

Map Ref
SX757809

MANATON

Freeland's Tower

Freeland's Tower is neither a folly nor a prospect tower, of which there are several in Devon, and for which this has often been mistaken.

Built around 1900 by Captain 'Daddy' White, a retired master mariner, the tower was employed as an astronomical observatory. Set on top of a low hill surrounded by massive rocks, the windowless tower stands 35ft tall and is 12ft in diameter. The observatory at the top was enclosed by a hemispherical glass dome, which housed the telescope. Records of the observations taken by Captain White are held by the Royal Astronomical Society.

The tower is now in a rather sad state, for the oak staircase has rotted away and the glass dome has long gone. (The present owner is planning to make the tower weatherproof, with access to the top once again.) The telescope, however, has survived and is in the possession of the 'Old Captain's' descendants.

Known locally as White's Tower, it was last used as a lookout by the Home Guard during the Second World War. The garden, of which the tower is a part, is open to the public once a year for charity.

80

Map Ref
SX602506

MEMBLAND

Bull and Bear Lodge

The banker, Edward Baring, later Lord Revelstoke, bought the Membland Estate in 1877 and transformed it, even having his

own branch railway line! After losing his fortune early in the twentieth century, the house became derelict and was demolished in the 1950s, with all the elaborate domestic buildings – coach house, stables, blacksmiths shop, estate housing, etc., becoming desirable retirement homes. The laundry, with its tower, ventilating steeple and clock, became the home of the tobacco magnate, Mr Dunhill.

Edward Baring married Georgiana Bulteel of Flete, and to celebrate the joining of the two families, he had a lodge built where the two great estates met – Bull and Bear Lodge. On top of the two gate piers are the supporters of the two families – a Bull and a Bear.

The stock exchange term 'bull market' (speculation on a fall in the market) and 'bear market' (speculation on a rise), stemmed from the two banking families – the Barings and the Bulteels – exemplified by the Lodge's gateway.

MEMBURY

Membury's Other Church

81
Map Ref
ST275025

Nikolaus Pevsner says that St John's Church in Membury is Perpendicular in style with a taller and slimmer tower than is usual in Devon, and it is well worth a visit. He does not, however, mention Membury's little sister church at Rock, half a mile down the road.

Built in 1821 by John Beasley, the twelve-year-old son of James Beasley, the local blacksmith, it is a miniature replica of St John's. It is 12ft 9in long, 3ft 9in wide and 14ft to the top of the turreted tower; there are four gargoyles on the corners of the tower and the remains of a wrought-iron weather-vane. It once held a peal of five bells, which John is reputed to have rung by himself – two with his hands, two with his feet and the fifth with his mouth.

There is also an inscribed stone: JB AD MDCCCXXI. Once standing beside a rough track leading up to fields, it has since been incorporated into the rear garden of the nearby cottage, and although now behind hedges, it can be glimpsed from the road and the field opposite.

Membury's other church.

82

MEMBURY

A Wartime Secret

High on Bewley Down, during the dark days of 1940–2, was a secret wireless station officially known as an Auxiliary Units Operations Base (OB).

It was one of many such stations scattered across the country to provide information from behind enemy lines should there be a successful German invasion and occupation of some of the country. The wireless 'net' that the Bewley Down station was on had its control at Castle Neroche Farm.

At the bottom of a cottage garden were two back-to-back earth-closet privies – or so they would appear. In one of the 'privies' the wooden seat, surround and bucket could be raised vertically on a steel frame by means of counterweights on pulleys. When raised, this revealed a narrow shaft with a ladder leading down into a low passage which then led into a concrete antechamber 5ft × 4ft × 6ft high, with an earthenware pipe in the ceiling which led to five concealed ventilators on the outside. To one side of the antechamber was a 6ft-square room constructed of curved sections of corrugated steel on low concrete walls, the far wall constructed from old railway sleepers. Against one wall was a hinged, wooden bench/bed and attached to the railway sleepers, a hinged table. However, the two sleepers to which the table was attached were hinged at the top and could swing forward and up, revealing a secret, similar-sized wireless room beyond. The

The privy and way down.

The living quarters with wireless room behind. Note the railway sleeper wall.

little complex was wired for electricity connected to the cottage, with a bank of batteries as back-up. The wireless aerials were concealed in the topmost branches of two Scots pines in a nearby spinney, with their leads hidden in the rough bark of their trunks. The earth-closet could be raised from below on receipt of a code given by an electric buzzer, the bell-push for which was concealed by a climbing plant near the cottage. It could also be opened from above, for one of the coat hooks on the wall of the privy was hinged, and if pushed up, activated the counterweights to raise the earth-closet.

Such was the secrecy of this station's construction that the Royal Engineer sappers who built it were brought daily from their camp in closed trucks, ensuring that they would have no idea of its exact location. When completed, the station was manned by two ATS subalterns who lived as civilians with the family at the cottage (the owner being a retired major in Army Intelligence and special constable).

There was a highly organised method of getting information (German troop movements, their units, etc.) to the wireless station, involving a network of local couriers, none of whom knew the identity of his (or her) fellow couriers. The messages were left in special 'drops' at the end of each stage. The last drop was a split-open tennis ball dropped down a tube in a bank hidden in the roots of a tree in the hedge surrounding the spinney. This tube was inclined and the ball dropped directly into the wireless room. Although this reads like a story from *Boy's Own*, it was a deadly serious operation in preparation for an eventuality which, happily, never occurred. Had it happened, then few of these Auxiliary Unit members would have survived for long.

Except for the removal of the wireless equipment, this OB remains much as it was in 1942. It remains private and is not open to the public.

83
Map Ref
SX658517

MODBURY

Scientific and Literary Institute

On Brownston Street, standing some way back from the road on the right-hand side, is an unusual and rather imposing building with

a heavy Tuscan porch and Doric columns to the upper floor.

This is now Kingsland House, once the home of the Modbury Scientific and Literary Institute, given to the townspeople of Modbury by Richard King, a native of Modbury who had emigrated to New York and made his fortune there. It was given so that everyone should have access to 'library and lecture facilities', but Richard King made certain stipulations: 'No discussion or lecture should include any subject that was likely to excite anger, or passion, or a fractious party split', which didn't really leave much to talk about – especially as the party is not specifically mentioned! The institute was closed in 1954 and became a private property.

84
Map Ref
SS743209

MONKLEIGH

Beam Bridge

The Rolle, or Torrington Canal was financed solely by Denys, Lord Rolle, so needing no parliamentary authority, with James Green as surveyor and engineer.

The aqueduct's arches over the River Taw.

It commenced from a river-lock on the River Torridge, just below Weare Gifford, and after being elevated by an inclined plane, followed the west bank of the river before crossing to the other side, via an aqueduct, to finish a mile above Great Torrington; a total length of a little over 6 miles. It opened in 1823 and closed in 1870 with the coming of the railway from Bideford to Torrington, which used the former course of the canal for some miles.

The five-arched, 23ft-wide aqueduct, with its Classical masonry, on which the canal had crossed the Torridge 55ft above the water, soon found another use; the iron trough of the canal was filled in and it became part of a new driveway to Beam House (now an activity centre). This not only provided a more direct access to the Bideford road, but gave an impressive approach to the house, with views up and down the wooded banks of the River Torridge from the bridge. As it was elegantly put at the time, 'Where once the horse-drawn tub-boats slowly glided now coaches go swiftly o'er'.

NORTH BOVEY

An Ash-House

85

Map Ref
SX710825

The ash-house at West Combe Farm is one of the best preserved in the country – with many other circular ones surviving on farms around Dartmoor. These were important features of agricultural farming methods until well into the twentieth century, for when spread on the land, wood ash, or any ash of an organic nature, provided it with potash, a valuable way of releasing nutrients in light or acid soils.

The ash had to be spread dry to allow the rain (of which Dartmoor has up to 80in a year) to wash it in. Farmhouses and other dwellings relied on wood, faggots of brushwood and furze (gorse), not only for warmth but for all water-heating and cooking on their open hearths, so a great deal of ash was made throughout the year, and had to be kept dry until needed.

Nearly hidden by its camouflage of vegetation.

This particular circular ash-house probably dates from the seventeenth century, and like the farm and its buildings, is made of granite, with its domed roof over the years having become covered with vegetation and turf. On the side most accessible to the farmhouse is a small opening through which the daily ash could be shot, with a door on the other side from which the ash could be drawn for spreading.

NORTH BRENTOR

Brent Tor

The little church of St Michael de la Rupe (St Michael of the Rock) sits perched on top of an isolated granite tor, and at 1,100ft, is a landmark that can be seen from miles around.

Built in 1130 by the Gifford family, Lords of the Manor of Lamerton, it is really tiny – only 37ft × 15ft with a 32ft tall tower. On one side its walls are only 3ft from the precipitous cliff and the other sides are enclosed by a low wall – a churchyard is hardly the name to apply as the ground is so 'thin' as to make burials difficult. In 1625, Tristram Risdon referred to it as 'a church full bleak and weather beaten, all alone as if it were forsaken'. But in fact it was never forsaken as it is the parish church of North Brent and although a new church was built in the village in the nineteenth century (to spare the infirm and elderly the steep climb), services are still held at regular intervals in the little church.

Church spires signified a reaching up to Heaven, so building a church on top of such a prominence had the same meaning, although there are stories connected with its building. One was that the church was to have been built at the foot of the tor, but every night the stones that had been laid were taken up to the top by the Devil, so in the end, to spite him, the church was built where it is. When it was completed the Archangel Gabriel threw the Devil over the precipice, so frightening him that he never returned.

There is, however, an extreme oddity about its position; whether one believes in ley lines or not, the church lies on a straight line between St Michael's Mount in Cornwall, through Burrow Mump and Glastonbury Tor in Somerset, Avebury in Wiltshire through to Caistor-on-Sea in Norfolk. This is the longest ley line in England and all the churches on or near it are dedicated to St Michael.

NEWTON ABBOT

The Dream Church

87

Map Ref
SX873701

During the 1930s, Newton Abbot expanded south-eastwards, with large estates built up the hill towards Milber Woods. Situated some way from the town's churches, a new parish was created with its own vicar (who was also the vicar of the neighbouring parish of Coffinswell). He was the Revd J. Keble Martin and he disliked having to take services in the little corrugated-iron Mission Church.

One night he had a vivid dream in which he envisioned a new church, and the next day recorded his dream in detail, determined to make his dream come true. He approached his brother, Arthur Martin, an architect, who drew up plans closely following those in Keble Martin's dream; eventually the money was raised and the church, St Luke's, was built. It was consecrated shortly before the war in 1939, but only completed in 1963.

The church is not the most beautiful in Devon, but it is certainly the most unusual. The building is 1,000in long, 1,000in wide and 1,000in high, with three naves converging on the stone altar like an arrowhead; there are three west doors and a squat crossing tower with a pyramidal copper roof. The north-eastern Lady Chapel also has a stone altar which was used from 1936 until the main body of the church was completed.

The Revd Keble Martin is better known for his *Flora Britannica*, one of the finest collections of wildflower paintings ever published.

The West Front.

NEWTON ABBOT

88
Map Ref
SX865917

A Boat on Wheels

The River Teign was used as a convenient way of transporting goods, especially ball- and china clay, down to the port of Teignmouth, with its own particular type of sailing barge. Newton Abbot was not accessible to these, even though it was on a little tributary, the River Lemon, which was not navigable except at very high tides. Where the little river became too shallow for the barges, its bed was paved and it was proposed that the smaller barges should be provided with little wheels so enabling them to be brought up further into the town. At low tide, the remains of this paving can be seen on the bed of the river. There is no firm evidence of wheels ever being fitted but they did go as far as the drawing board and it was a good idea anyway!

A typical Teign clay barge, *c.* 1880, and a wheeled version for the Lemon.

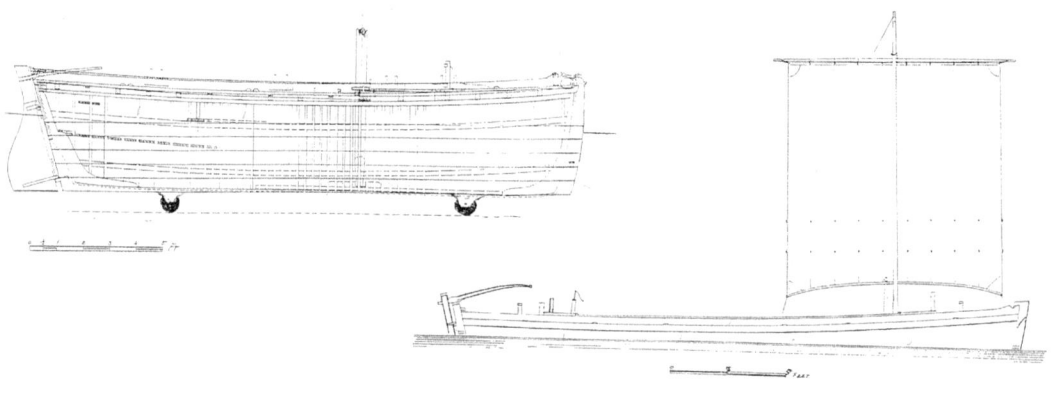

NEWTON POPPLEFORD

89
Map Ref
SY077895

Not a Talking Clock!

If you travel into Newton Poppleford from Exeter, keep a lookout to the right. Standing in front of a house is a clock – but not just any old clock. When the Post Office was selling off many of its famous red phone boxes, the owner of the house bought one as a garden ornament – that is, until he acquired a large clock face and movement, found in an attic in North Devon; its size indicating that it must once have belonged to a public clock. The phone box made the perfect case for the clock – the face being as wide as the box and the pendulum as long as the height of the box. A popular tourist attraction, the clock keeps perfect time and is a delightful piece of recycling! The village name, Newton Poppleford, means 'a new homestead by the dancing waters of a ford'.

NORTH MOLTON

Upwardly Mobile

North Molton was a prosperous cloth-making centre using wool from local sheep, and although during the fifteenth century it was still a cottage industry, the trade was becoming highly organised by the wool merchants and clothiers. In about 1525, Thomas Parker was one such merchant living in a comfortable and substantial house in the centre of the small town of North Molton, opposite the church. On a gable, he had a plaque bearing his monogram, or cipher, which he used as a 'wool mark' stamped on his bales of wool or cloth. Both house and plaque are still there.

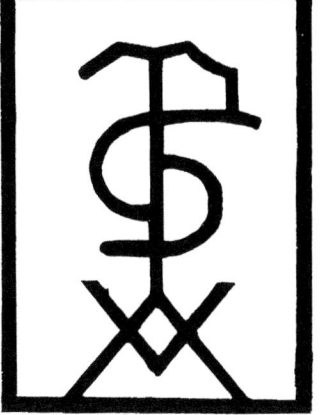

His son married an heiress, Elizabeth Frye, of Hatherleigh, thus starting the family's upwardly social progress, and they later became the Earls of Morley, purchasing the large and imposing mansion, Saltram House, near Plymouth, in 1712. Over three generations, they made it one of the grandest houses in Devon, with luxurious furniture, paintings and fittings. Today it is owned by the National Trust.

Parker's home in North Molton. Note the 'woolmark'.

91
Map Ref
SS654003

NORTH TAWTON

le Bathe Pool

The Revd Thomas Fuller, writing on Devonshire history, industries and customs in his book *The Worthys of England* (1664) related the following tale from North Tawton: 'In this parish near a house called Bathe [now le Bathe Barton] there is a pit . . . in the winter a pool not maintained by any spring but by rain. Before the death of any Prince, or of some other strange accident of great importance, it will in a hot or dry season without rain overflow its banks, and so continue till it be past that it prognosticated'.

The pit at le Bathe remains today and heavy rainwater collects at the bottom, but only after a period of exceptionally heavy rain does it fill completely – every eight to ten years or so – before eventually seeping away. Local legend says that it filled before the deaths of Nelson in 1805, Wellington in 1852, Edward VII in 1910 and at the commencement of the First World War in 1914. These were in all probability coincidental, and no noteworthy dates have been recorded recently, although the 'pool' has occasionally filled up.

But this does not detract from the peculiar nature of the pool, and although there must be a logical, possibly geological explanation, this has yet to be discovered. The 'pool' is a circular-shaped bowl measuring about 100ft across and 10ft deep at the centre. It is grass covered and there are no rushes or any sign of a damp area at the bottom. In the summer there is no evidence of it ever having held water, but it is of such a size to warrant it being shown by the slope symbol on the OS 1:50,000 map.

The area is now protected by English Heritage, not because of the 'pool', but its adjacent Roman vexillation fort, which held a garrison of 1,000 or so men. This was discovered by crop marking shown on aerial photography and proved subsequently by archaeological digs.

Below: The grass-lined 'pool'.

Bottom: A rare view of the pool filled up, *c.* 1990. *(John Shields)*

OFFWEL

Bishop Coplestone's Folly

92
Map Ref
ST183004

Anyone driving westward along the A35 cannot fail to notice a tall tower on the left about 2 miles before reaching Honiton. It was built, together with a row of cottages, between 1842 and 1847 by the Bishop of Llandaff, the Very Revd Edward Coplestone, who lived in the house nearby, to provide work for the great number of unemployed in the area. It is 70ft to the viewing platform, 80ft to the cupola, both of which are leaded and surrounded by wrought-iron railings, and 100ft to the top of the weather-vane. The first three floors are reached by a circular staircase in its south-western corner and the last two by wooden steps. In the early 1900s, a water tank was installed on the fourth floor, giving rise to the popular belief that the tower was built for that sole purpose. The name Bishop Coplestone's Folly stemmed from the after-dinner story that the good Bishop was fond of telling – that he built the tower so that he could keep an eye on his flock in his diocese in Wales.

But why did the Bishop of Llandaff have a home in Offwell? Coming from a very old Devonshire family, he loved the county and had been Rector of Offwell before being elevated to Bishop.

OTTERY ST MARY

The Astronomical Clock

93
Map Ref
SY099956

With the exception of Exeter Cathedral, St Mary's is arguably the finest ecclesiastical building in Devon – a cathedral in miniature – but Nicholas Pevsner thinks nothing of it! Unfortunately, as with so many churches, much of its beautiful decoration and stained glass was destroyed, while effigies were defaced in the savagery of the Dissolution and the Civil War (1642–6), when General Fairfax and the Parliamentarians occupied Ottery St Mary. This in no way detracts from the splendour of the fabric of the church, and there remains one superb survivor – the Astronomical Clock.

Built between 1327 and 1369, when the earth was still thought to be the centre of the universe, the theory propounded by Ptolemy, it has a square face with an outer circle showing the 24-hour day in Roman numerals, with the hour being indicated by a golden sun which moves clockwise within the circle, the minutes having to be interpolated. The inner circle has thirty discs with Arabic numerals, with a star revolving on its outer rim to show the age of the moon. Within this circle is a

The clock face in St Mary's.

black and white orb which revolves on its own axis to show the phases of the moon, travelling around the circle once every 24 hours. In the very centre is the earth, around which everything revolves. There are three other similar clocks in the West Country – at Exeter, Wells and Wimborne Minster – but this is the only one worked by its largely original mechanism, making it one of the oldest surviving clocks in the country.

Another more visible object survived Fairfax's attention – just! This is the great copper 'whistling' weathercock on top of the spire, so-called because it has two tubes inserted into its body which whistle in the wind. When Fairfax was in Ottery St Mary, the weathercock was used by his men as a target for musket practice, with several balls piercing the tail. Some years ago, the cock was taken down for renovation and was given a new tail; the original holey tail is now displayed under glass in the church. The 'whistles' were also repaired, but their noise upset local residents and they had to be quietened.

OTTERY ST MARY

94

Map Ref
SY095953

Tumbling Weir

Water-powered mills invariably have a relief weir of some sort, either to carry excess water away from the water-wheel or as a protection in times of flood.

In 1790, a large serge mill was built to the west of the town, taking water for the water-wheel from the River Otter via a leat. However, because there was a lane leading to another property immediately adjacent and below the head pond above the mill, it was not possible to have a conventional weir and spillway back to the river.

The most ingenious, and unique, solution to the problem was to have a circular weir in the centre of the head-pond, with its edge just below the water level when the mill was not working. Water flows over the outer edge of the 10ft diameter of the weir on to

a concentric ledge about 3ft below before being discharged down a vertical pipe into a tunnel beneath the mill and thence into the mill's tail race and back into the river.

It is a fascinating spectacle which can be clearly seen from the footpath alongside the leat, reached from that same lower lane, but which now leads to the Tumbling Weir Hotel.

OTTERY ST MARY

On 5 November

95
Map Ref
SY099954

Several towns in England celebrate Guy Fawkes night on 5 November in an individual way; Lewis, in Sussex parade effigies through the streets and at Bridgwater in Somerset, men hold giant squibs above their heads. Ottery St Mary hosts two unique events – firing the rock-cannon and rolling the blazing tar barrels.

At 5.30 a.m., the town is awoken by a fusillade of explosions from rock-cannons, which continue at intervals until 7 a.m., succeeded by further firings from different locations and by different participants (about forty in number, all aged sixteen or over) between 1 and 2 p.m., 4 and 5 p.m., and 7 and 7.30 p.m. The small 'cannons' are held in the right hand by a 7in-long steel handle which then bends at about 140 per cent to form the 7in barrel, bored out to 1⅛in to a depth of 31in. There is a percussion nipple which holds the 'cap' and the cannon is discharged by striking the nipple with a metal striker held in the left hand. The powder used is made in America for muzzle-loading muskets, but formerly gunpowder was used for blasting rock, hence the name 'rock cannons'. Stringent precautions are taken over loading, priming and firing the cannons; the first recorded explosion was in 1802, carried out by schoolboys. The first special handheld cannons were made by the local blacksmith and were bell-mouthed, probably simple copies of the old blunderbuss. The custom had to cease with the Second World War in 1939 but was revived in 1956.

Firing the 'cannons'.
(A. Nelson Owen)

A flaming
tar-barrel.
*(David Riley,
c. 2006)*

'Rolling' tar-barrels is a misnomer, for the blazing barrels are carried on the shoulders of the runners, who are protected solely by wet sacking and having their head and hair liberally coated with Vaseline. The flames blaze out of the open-ended barrels, and once the runners start, it is up to the spectators to get out of their way, which often leads to a mad scramble in the narrow streets!

The 'rolling' commences at 4 p.m. with small barrels carried by boys aged between 7 and 12; teenagers run at 7 p.m. and the men start at 7.30 p.m., the runs continuing until after 10 p.m.

No one seems to know how or why this custom originated but it has been suggested that the first blazing barrels held sulphur, to fumigate the town after an epidemic. How this became associated with Guy Fawkes is also unknown but this in no way detracts from this time-honoured spectacle.

PLYMOUTH

96
Map Ref
SX470504

Breakwater

Devonport and its dockyard were well protected both defensively and from the elements, being well up the Hamoaze, as the Rivers Tamar, Tavy and Lynher became before entering Plymouth Sound. Plymouth and the Sound itself were protected from the west by Penlee Point and from the east by Wembury Point, but was wide open to the south, both to the weather and during the Napoleonic Wars, to enemy warships.

A map of
Plymouth
Breakwater from
an encyclopedia
of around 1850.

It was decided to build a breakwater across the middle of the Sound to make it a safer anchorage and also to bring any vessel entering it within range of guns on shore. It would be built on shallower water known as Shovel Shoal and was to be a mile in length, with John Rennie as the designer. Construction commenced in 1812 and after John's death in 1822, it was completed by his son, Sir John Rennie, in 1842. With the top being 20ft above high water, the breakwater needed 3,000,000 tons of Oreston limestone to build it using specially-constructed boats to bring it to the site. The surface was finished with dressed granite from Cornwall and Dartmoor, with a lighthouse at the western end and a beacon at the other; the fort in the middle was not built until 1861–8. When one considers that all the stone had to be quarried by hand, transported to the boats in horse-drawn wagons and then laid in position, it is no wonder that the breakwater took thirty years to build, and goodness knows how many lives.

97

Map Ref
SX471536

PLYMOUTH

The Custom House

After the South Devon Railway Co. ran a branch line to Millbay harbour and pier, a new phase of Plymouth's nautical history began which continued until the 1960s, only ending with the advent of air travel. The large and luxurious steam liners on the transatlantic route would call in to Millbay harbour and pier, with mail and passengers being transferred to express trains for the onward journey to London (and vice versa), thus saving many hours in travelling time.

A passenger terminus with its own railway station, warehouses and the Pier Hotel were established at Millbay. The octagonal, three-storey Custom House was built in 1850, designed by George Wightwick, and is today the only original building which survives, all the rest being swept away when the harbour became a marina.

98

Map Ref
SX450533

PLYMOUTH

To a Pig

This particular curiosity is a bit of a cheat, for the memorial is not in Plymouth and not even in Devon, but in Cornwall. It is, however, in a country park owned by Plymouth City Council and can be viewed more easily from Plymouth than anywhere else. Seen from Mount Wise or Stonehouse, the elegant 30ft-high obelisk which overlooks the Hamoze might naturally be taken for a monument to a famous figure from Plymouth's nautical history – but it is in fact a monument to a pig!

It was erected in the second half of the eighteenth century by the Countess of Mount Edgecumbe in memory of her faithful companion, her pet pig, Cupid. Cupid would loyally follow the Countess around like a dog, coming in to meals and even accompanying her on her visits to London.

When Cupid died, he was interred close to Mount Edgecumbe House and according to a newspaper report, was 'Buried in a gold casket, the spot being marked, on the instruction of the Countess, by an obelisk'. This event did not escape the notice of that great eighteenth-century satirist and writer of scurrilous verse, Dr John Wolcot, better known as Peter Pindar, who wrote:

> O dry that tear so round and big,
> Not waste in sighs your precious wind,
> Death only takes a single pig –
> Your Lord and son are left behind.

The obelisk was moved from the grounds of Mount Edgecumbe House to its present site in the 1860s. Incidentally, Dr John Wolcot was a Devonian; born and educated at Kingsbridge.

SALCOMBE REGIS

The Thorn

99
Map Ref
S148891

At the top of the lane leading down to the hamlet of Salcombe Regis and its church of St Mary and St Peter is a triangular piece of ground in which there is an inscribed stone and a thorn tree. The stone was erected in 1939 by Vaugham Cornish and Christopher Tomkinson, trustees of the Thorn Estate, and records the ancient nature of the thorn and its significance: 'A thorn tree has been maintained her Saxon times when it marked the boundary between the cultivated fields of the combe and the open common of the bill. It has given its name to the adjacent house, part of which is pre-Reformation, where the manor court was held, and to the surrounding farm'.

On moorland and other waste ground, the thorn tree, due to its longevity and resistance to storms and salt air, was often used as a boundary marker, although it is more often only the name that has survived. In this case, of course, the tree would have been replaced many times.

The little brick building with its iron-barred door a quarter of a mile east of the thorn is not, in spite of its appearance, a lockup but a well-house and throw-pump – the iron door was a later addition. It was erected in 1884 as a memorial to the Revd T. Anderson Moorhead, vicar at Salcombe Regis. The well is now 126ft 9in deep, having to have been deepened in 1892 following a severe drought.

SANDFORD

A Classical Education

Sandford Primary School fronts on to the village street but on a much higher level, above a sheer retaining wall with iron railings, reached by stone steps – and what a frontage it has! Six Classical Greek columns support a pediment proudly proclaiming its name and date – SANDFORD SCHOOL MDCCCXXV. It was provided by Sir John Davie, the ninth Baronet, of nearby Creedy House, who was born in 1798. It is probably the only primary school in the country with Classical Greek architecture, and was built by three local craftsmen, William Edwards (mason), John Eme (carpenter) and John Kendell (sculptor), working not from plans but from a model of the building, which the school proudly possesses. Above the inscription was the Davie family's coat of arms, the paschal lamb, carved in relief below the pediment, together with the names of the three craftsmen. When the building underwent extensive repairs in the 1950s, the relief and names were done away with, the open, colonnaded arcade enclosed and plain glass substituted for the stained glass depicting the Seven Virtues in the front windows.

Devon cottages are renowned for their cob walls (compressed earth, clay or chalk reinforced with straw) which, as well as being cheap, are extremely durable if kept dry. It is hardly surprising, therefore, that in this rural area, cob should have been used in the school's construction. What is unusual is that the walls are the tallest in the country to be built with cob – which says a lot for those old craftsmen!

Above: The model of Sandford School, high on a shelf out of the children's reach!

Sandford School, 2007.

It is possible that Sir John had been on the Grand Tour (the war with France then being over) which had influenced his choice of architecture. The property remained with the Davie family until 1937. Whatever its history, this Grade II listed building is truly eye catching and a unique school.

SEATON

The Stop Line of 1940

101
Map Ref
SY255898

With the very real threat of a German invasion anywhere along the south coast, should they land west of Seaton, it was important that any thrust eastwards be slowed down. A defensive line was therefore built across the waist of South West England, from Seaton to the mouth of the River Parrett in Somerset. Existing physical features such as rivers, canals and railways formed the basis of the line and from Seaton to Weycroft (ST306000), this was the River Axe. All bridges could be blown up but the river could easily be forded by vehicles and troops; so a great number of gun-emplacements, pillboxes and anti-tank barriers were built along the east bank of the river, all positioned facing westwards. Some 215 of these concrete structures have survived out of over 350 built along the whole line and many

A 6in-gun emplacement covering the River Axe.

of those along the Axe can still easily be seen, although in 1940 they would have been elaborately camouflaged.

Additionally, there was an ill-thought-out scheme to flood the lower reaches of the river, to make crossing it even more difficult. This involved building two earth dams across it near its mouth; one opposite the railway station and the other below the bridge. The power of the river and the weight of the pounded water soon breached these and the idea was abandoned. Today, all that can be seen is a stump of the earth dam jutting out from the shingle bank just below the marina.

Anti-tank blocks at Weycroft.

102

Map Ref
SY253899

SEATON

The Toll Bridge

Until 130 years ago, the first bridge over the River Axe was 2 miles upstream at Axe Bridge on the main Exeter to Dorchester road (A3052). The rough road from Axmouth to Axmouth harbour was partially tidal and at very low tides, it was possible for carts to ford the river a couple of hundred yards from its mouth, with pedestrians ferried across from the harbour.

The coming of the railway to Seaton in 1868 prompted a local landowner, Sir William Trevelyan, to commission Phillip Brennon to design and build a bridge across the river near the railway station, in 1875. Although Brennon was later to become an exponent of building with reinforced concrete, this bridge was built of mass concrete, with indented ornamentation to make it look as though it was of traditional stone construction. There are three spans, two at 30ft and the centre one at 50ft, and the bridge was lit by gas lamps, two being mounted centrally on the parapets. It was opened in 1877 and is the oldest mass concrete bridge in the country. The little single-storey tollhouse (Sir William was not a philanthropist) with its low, curving roof, is also built of concrete and is an early example of the use of this material for housing. Tolls ceased to be charged in 1907 and the tidal road to Axmouth was raised to its present level in 1928 (no doubt the coming of the automobile had something to do with this!)

The bridge in 1901. Note the tidal road opposite.

SHALDON

The Ness Tunnel

The Ness (from the French *nez*, meaning nose) is a high, wooded promontory to the west of the mouth of the River Teign, effectively cutting off the village of Shaldon from the open sea. Built on the site of a former farmhouse in about 1830, Ness House overlooked Teignmouth but had no access to the sea; the estate did, however, include a sheltered, sandy cove to the west of the Ness, but this was relatively inaccessible due to steep cliffs. There had been a tunnel leading from the old farm directly to the beach, but this had been blocked by several rock falls. This tunnel had been reputedly used by smugglers.

The new owner of the estate, therefore, had a level tunnel dug from near his home to a belvedere high on the cliff overlooking the Ness beach, with a flight of steps going down to the shore. Because the rock through which this tunnel was dug was soft, it was lined with stonework and was just wide enough to take a bath chair or a pony chaise. In 1940, when a German invasion seemed imminent, the steps down the cliff were blown up and the entrance blocked off with concrete.

In 1949, the Ness Estate was purchased by Teignmouth Council who, recognising the advantage of having a more sheltered beach, decided to reopen the tunnel. A short stretch of the tunnel leading to the Belvedere was blocked off and a new tunnel dug, with internal stone steps which were completed in 1952, thus making the beach accessible to holidaymakers and walkers.

The Ness, Ness House and beacon light in 1851. (Illustrated London News)

The new exit and steps are on the right, with the old 'smugglers' tunnel' exit in the centre.

Although not as grand or as wide as the tunnels at Ilfracombe, this tunnel is far longer and is free. The beach entrance to the old 'smugglers' tunnel' still exists and is currently used as a store for deckchairs.

104
Map Ref
SS438092

SHEBBEAR

The Devil's Stone

Lying on the Green at Shebbear is a large sarsen stone, known as the Devil's Stone, one of several such stones in the area and weighing over a ton. It was once positioned in front of the lych-gate of St Michael's Church, but in the 1920s or '30s, because more vehicles were being used by those attending services, funerals and weddings, it was moved to its present position – on 5 November, naturally!

According to custom, after sunset on the evening of 5 November, a peal of bells is rung at the church. The bell ringers then come out and, with crowbars, ceremoniously turn the stone over, after which another peal is rung. The stone is turned in the old belief that the Devil won't recognise it and sit on it during the coming year. No one knows when, why or how this custom arose, nor why it is carried out on 5 November although this is probably because 'bond-fire night', as it was first called, has traditionally been a night of jollification and merriment.

The Devil's Stone.

Many of those who now help turn the stone today are following in their father's and grandfather's footsteps, and repair afterwards to the Devil's Stone Inn, named the New Inn in the 1960s.

SHUTE

Shute Pillars

On an acute turn on the road from Seaton Cross to Seaton Junction, about a mile from the handsome gatehouse to Shute House and Barton, are two tall stone pillars, each topped with a stone ball – one on each side of the road. These pillars were built long before the turnpike road was constructed and so would have directly faced the old Axminster to Honiton road, flanking what was in fact a country lane leading eventually to Colyton, but would have appeared to make a rather grand entrance to the Shute Estate! No exact date can be given to the pillars, but over the years they

have received the attention of 'vandals' carving their initials and dates; the earliest being 'H.L., 1711' on one, and 'T.S., 1743' on the other.

SIDBURY

'Boney' or the Devil

There were two menaces facing the worshippers at St Giles Church in Sidbury at the beginning of the nineteenth century; the threat of a French invasion, feared by all, or being taken by the Devil, feared by some.

The powder room over the south porch.

Elaborate plans were prepared should Napoleon Bonaparte ('Boney') invade this part of Devon; wagons and carts were organised to take women, children and the elderly to safer areas inland, each family having a card telling them which wagon or cart they were allocated and instructing them to take blankets and two days' food. The carters had to have a spare set of shoes for their horses and were told to keep to the back lanes so avoiding the turnpike roads, leaving them clear for military traffic. The men were organised into a local militia and issued with muskets, the gunpowder for which was stored in a little room above the south porch of St Giles Church; this was the 'Powder Room', still known as such today. The younger women would have to parade on the cliff tops dressed in their traditional, red woollen winter cloaks in an attempt to dupe the French into believing that there were Redcoats waiting to repel them!

A spiked tomb.

The Devil was another matter, for many believed that he would try and catch them as they emerged from their graves on Resurrection Day. They were especially vulnerable just as they emerged, so it was important to ensure that Old Nick wouldn't be waiting for them close by. The chest tomb of the Newman family had sharp iron spikes set closely around the tomb's stone cover, and in the same churchyard, there are six gravestones having similar spikes set along their top edges, so making it too painful for the Devil to sit on them and pounce as their souls came out! The cynic

might claim that the Newmans didn't want layabouts or children sitting or playing on their tomb – but that doesn't explain about the spiked gravestones!

SIDMOUTH

107

Map Ref
SY28874

Crossing the Sid

There are far too many handsome and picturesque buildings in Sidmouth to single one out – they have, in any case, all been written about, photographed and eulogised too many times already. Before it became a fashionable watering place in the late eighteenth century, Sidmouth had been a small fishing village clustered along the west bank of the little River Sid. The direct way of crossing the river if going east was by way of a ford or water splash, as it would then have been called. It is still in use today, unless the river is in flood, when a motorist can still find himself immobilised if not careful. Cyclists are still warned not to attempt the crossing, even if it is one of the last water splashes remaining in Devon.

This, however, did not do for the emerging genteel classes living in Sidmouth, and in about 1817, a bridge was built a hundred yards upstream; but this had to be paid for, so a tollhouse was built to collect the fees. This is a delightful building designed in the Greek Revival style with a porch having four columns, a pediment and tall, tapered central chimneys. The gate itself is now hung across the entrance to a riverside walk.

Later in the century, visitors wanted more than just a promenade along the sea front; they wanted to see the view from the top of Sidmouth Hill but they didn't want to get their feet wet. So, to

Top: Alma Bridge; *above:* across the 'water splash' in safety.

commemorate that great Crimean battle of the Alma, a footbridge was built across the Sid in 1855 near its mouth – Alma Bridge.

SIDMOUTH

The Lockyer Observatory

108
Map Ref
SY139883

Sir Norman Lockyer (1836–1920) trained as a linguist but it wasn't until he bought his first 3½in telescope in about 1860, that his interest in astronomy blossomed. He joined the moon-mapping group under Warren de la Rue, and with a borrowed 6½in lens telescope, mapped the moon at four times the scale as had been done previously. The geographer, Dr Phillips, wrote, 'I am delighted with your drawings, the result of a good lens, good eyes and hands and a real love of the work . . .'

In 1868, the publishing house Macmillan brought out the now world-renowned scientific journal *Nature* with Lockyer as editor, a position he held for fifty years. However, Lockyer's greatest contribution to science was his work on the sun; he purchased a simple spectroscope and commenced to examine the solar spectrum (damaging his right eye in the process), during total eclipses of the sun. Edmund Frankland had collected the spectra of all the known elements, and this enabled Lockyer to identify the presence of sodium, barium, calcium and other chemical elements in the sun's makeup; but he also discovered one set of yellow lines which did not correspond with any known element, so Lockyer called it helium, after helios, the Greek word for the sun. It would, however, be another twenty-seven years before the element was discovered on earth. Imperial College was born out of the science laboratories at South Kensington, where the Solar Physics Laboratory was situated and where Lockyer, now Sir Norman, was Director. Due to smoke pollution in the City, the laboratory moved to Cambridge in 1909.

Sir Norman became President of the British Association in 1903, and after the laboratory's move to Cambridge, he commenced building his retirement home on Sidmouth Hill, overlooking the sea and the town to the west. But retirement was not in Sir Norman's nature, for he bequeathed to Devon a rare facility – an observatory.

From its conception it was not financed by the government or a university, but solely from Sir Norman's own resources and those of his friends. It is still fiercely independent, although it is greatly helped by the local East Devon District Council. It is one of only five observatories regularly open to the public – with over forty open days and evenings per year, as well as hosting school parties from all over the county.

Building started on rough heathland above Lockyer's home, and it initially sported a dome for his faithful old 6½in telescope and a bungalow, the Long House, to house the library, records and laboratories. The First World World delayed its completion, but when Sir Norman died in 1920 he had had the foresight to make

The main buildings and planetarium.

it a Corporation, with his son James carrying on as Director. A 10in Grunn refractor was given by Sir Norman's close friend, Francis McClean, and another refractor came from the old Solar Physics Laboratory. Today there is a lecture theatre and a sixty-seat planetarium with current equipment for the reception of images of the earth from weather satellites, meteorology and radio astronomy. It is now a charity.

Lockyer's old 6in telescope.

The observatory is a fitting memorial to Sir Norman's contribution to science – as founder of the Science Museum, the creation of Imperial College and his groundbreaking work on the sun. But perhaps his greatest gift to the scientific community was the journal, Nature.

Further information on the laboratory's opening times can be obtained by calling 01395 579941.

The Mond Dome.

SLAPTON

Slapton Sands

109
Map Ref
SX826420–
SX840465

Like the Chesil Bank in Dorset, the shingle ridge of Slapton Sands, extending from Torcross to Pilchard Cove with a smaller beach at Beesands, was formed at the end of the last ice age when the English Channel was the mouth of a huge river. It also shelves steeply into the sea and has a lake on its landward side, but here the similarity ends for Slapton is only 4 miles long – 6 miles if Beesands is included – and the lake or 'ley' as it is called, is freshwater, fed by three small streams, and

Slapton Sands, looking east from Torcross. *(Author's Collection)*

percolates through the shingle to the sea. There is another difference, for whereas the length of Chesil is graduated from shingle to large pebbles, Slapton Sands is wholly shingle. For centuries, it was a place of peace and solitude used only by fishermen, both in the sea and the Ley, and more recently by ornithologists, for once even bitterns used to breed in the Ley's reed beds. The road that runs along the top of the shingle ridge is the most convenient route from Dartmouth to Kingsbridge and travellers were catered for by the Royal Sands Hotel, built on the seaward side of the road opposite the causeway across the Ley leading to Slapton village. The hotel acquired its 'Royal' from King Edward VII who once frequented it.

Christmas 1943 saw the end of Slapton's peace and solitude, for the area became the training ground for American forces in preparation for the beach landings in France. They had to train under battle conditions, with live artillery and naval barrages, landing craft, tanks and the whole paraphernalia of modern warfare. The entire population of the area extending from Torcross to Blackpool Sands and extending some 10 miles inland, had to leave. This involved 3,000 people, 840 households, and over 200 entire farms with thousands of livestock, and not forgetting the crops still in the ground. They were given under two months to clear out and it was ten months before they could return to their battle-scarred houses and buildings and shell-blasted woods and hedgerows. Today, the only reminder of this upheaval and destruction is a Sherman tank at Torcross, retrieved from the sea, and a memorial, greatly damaged in a recent gale, on the spot where the Royal Sands Hotel once stood, blown up by the Americans and never rebuilt.

Between Torcross and Beesands, the 2-mile long beach has another reedy ley behind it, which enjoys greater solitude because there is no road between it and the sea.

Slapton Sands is not favoured as a holiday destination, as the steeply shelving beach is really only safe for good swimmers, and the shingle, though comfortable to sit and walk on, is not suitable for

The Ley and causeway to Slapton village and the Royal Sands Hotel, *c.* 1930.

building sandcastles! It does, however, have a place in the history of naturism in this country, for Pilchard Cove, at the extreme eastern end of the beach, was one of the few beaches in Britain before the war, where a blind eye was turned on nudists, and this area, now extended, continues to be used by nudists today.

SOUTH BRENT

The Market

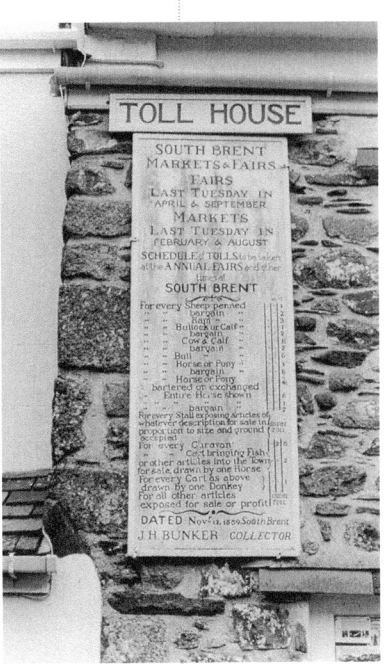

Most small towns had market days held at regular intervals, and South Brent was no exception. There were two a year, held on the last Tuesday in February and August, with another two being added later, in April and September – Lamb Fair and Goose Fair respectively. Like other towns hosting infrequent markets, South Brent had no marketplace or field, so livestock was penned and sold in the streets, which must have caused a lot of disruption to what traffic there was, but must also have added to the atmosphere of the fair – in more ways than one!

The horses and ponies were penned in Station Road, with the cattle in Church Street. South Brent became known as the major centre for the sale of Dartmoor ponies (just as Bampton was for Exmoor ponies), most of which were destined for work in the Welsh coal mines, and it is recorded that in 1904, over 500 were transported from South Brent railway station. It is now hard to imagine their suffering – being taken from the freedom of the moor to working and living underground, with only brief respites in the open.

There is still a visible reminder of these markets in South Brent: in Church Street there is a little clock-cum-fire-bell tower which acted as a tollhouse when the market charges were collected. On the outside is a board, erected in 1889, detailing the charges for each animal brought into market and again on their sale, or 'bargain'. It is interesting to see that, as pony and horse sales always attracted gypsy traders, one of the tolls was for caravans, but where these were parked is not mentioned, nor if any tolls were successfully collected.

SOUTH ZEAL

The Menhir

There are many standing stones, or Menhirs, on Dartmoor, one of the largest and best known being near Merrivale (SX555745); but the one found in the village of South Zeal must be the strangest.

The Oxenham Arms, now a comfortable hotel, was first erected by lay monks at the end of the twelfth century, later becoming the Dower House of the Burgoyne family, before passing by marriage to the Oxenhams.

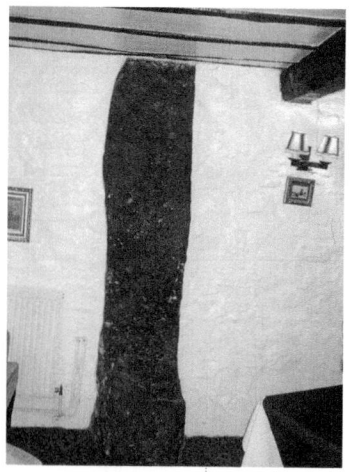

The site the lay monks chose for their inn included a standing stone, which they incorporated into the structure as part of a wall. So why include it? Why hide it from general view yet be fearful of destroying it? Were they playing it safe by having one foot in the new Christianity and the other in the pagan past?

Today, the stone forms part of the wall in the dining room of the hotel, standing sentinel over the excellent food offered up to the guests. Archaeologists have examined it and even dug down several feet to try and establish its height, but they were unable to get to the bottom of it – in more sense than one!

112
Map Ref
SX977818

STARCROSS

The Atmospheric Railway

Starcross pumphouse from the south with the truncated chimney on the right.

Between the narrow main street in Starcross and the river wall of the Exe is a large, rather ornate stone building with what looks like a tower on its river side which is, in fact, a truncated chimney. This steam pump house is the most visible remains of Isambard Kingdom Brunel's atmospheric railway, which he planned to run from Exeter to Plymouth, but which only got as far as Newton Abbot.

Contrary to popular belief, the atmospheric railway was not Brunel's idea, but was actually the brainchild of Messrs Clegg and Samunda, nor was it the first, that being at Croydon. Brunel, however, wholeheartedly believed in the system and decided to use it on his planned South Devon Railway.

The system was apparently a simple one: steam pumping stations situated every 3 miles or so would exhaust the air from a 15in iron pipe laid between the rails of the railway, on top of which was a longitudinal slot, sealed by a hinged iron and leather flap. A close-fitting piston inside the pipe was attached by a stanchion, going through the slot to the underside of the leading coach of the train. As air was exhausted in front of the piston, atmospheric pressure behind it forced it along. The stanchion opened the flap to allow forward movement and small wheels behind it closed the flap. The train could attain 17mph and the passengers enjoyed the smooth running and quietness, and lack of dust and fumes.

Unfortunately, the idea preceded the technology, for grease had to be used to perfect the seal (which rats ate), the leather flap was subject to damage from frost, water and heat, and there were severe technical problems when stopping at stations.

By the time the line was operating as far as Newton Abbot, Brunel realised that the difficulties were too great to continue and he reverted to conventional railway engines. The atmospheric railway opened in 1847 but closed within the year, so ending a grand experiment. Remains of other pumphouses are at Exeter (SX912932), Dawlish (SX964768) and Torre (SX901662) which was to have had a branch line.

STOCKLAND

A Warning

113
Map Ref
ST255054

Until 1833, Stockland parish was an 'island' of Dorset surrounded by Devonshire subject to Dorset's bylaws. An iron notice on a stone bridge over the River Yarty, at remote Longbridge, baldly states: 'DORSET. Any person wilfully INJURING any part of this COUNTY BRIDGE will be guilty of felony and upon conviction liable to be TRANSPORTED FOR LIFE. By the Court. T. Fooks. 7&8 Geo. AC 30 S13'. There is a similar notice on another bridge over the Yarty in Stockland village itself.

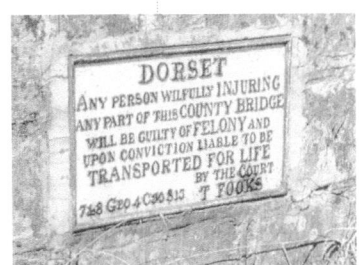

STOKE FLEMING

The Calculating Boy

114
Map Ref
SX863485

Fixed inconspicuously on the garden wall of Bidders, a house at the narrowest part of Stoke Fleming's notoriously narrow main street, is a circular, roughly-executed commemorative plaque to George Parker Bidder (1806–78), linking his name with Robert and George Stephenson, the railway prioneers. But what is really intriguing is the soubriquet given to George Parker – 'The Calculating Boy'.

George Bidder was born in Moretonhampstead, the son of a stone mason; he was not a scholar, and at the age of seven couldn't tell the time and didn't understand the meaning of the words, days, weeks, months and years, but once he knew the units each represented, he could instantly give an answer to any combination of them. His father saw financial gain in his prodigy and toured the country with him. On visiting Cambridge, Sir John Herschel saw his potential and paid for a tutor until George's father missed the income from touring!

George Bidder's plaque in Stoke Fleming.

Eventually, while in Edinburgh, Sir Henry Jardine prised George away, and from 1819–24, paid for him to attend university there. After a brief period with the Ordnance Survey, he became a civil and hydraulic engineer, responsible for Lowestoft Harbour and the Victoria and Blackwall wharves in London.

In 1834 he joined Robert and George Stephenson and represented them at parliamentary committees, when railway bills were being considered. His wonderful memory and almost instantaneous calculations were a tremendous asset. On one occasion there was a query regarding a line of levels presented by an opposing party. On asking to see their field books, Bidder looked at them in a cursory manner and immediately pointed out the error, going through the calculations of the entire line of levels without again referring to the books! The mind of any present-day surveyor would boggle at the thought of trying to work them out in his head – with a calculator it was tedious enough!

On one famous occasion, while before a committee in the House of Lords, the hostile lawyers complained that 'Mr Bidder should not be allowed to remain in the room, because Nature had endowed him with qualities that did not place his opponents on a fair footing'.

Bidder lived and worked all his life in London and the North of England, but retired to Warfleet, near Dartmouth, and is buried in the churchyard of St Peter at Stoke Fleming, where his family came to live and where he is commemorated.

TAPELEY PARK

The Ice House

Ice houses were introduced into Britain from France in the seventeenth century, and the ensuing popularity of iced creams and puddings, sorbets and cool drinks during the summer, meant that they became a must-have on many large estates (together with pineapples) to enhance their dinner tables. The South West was no exception, for examples can still be found at Bicton, Haccombe, Killerton and Tapeley Park.

Just as potatoes and other root crops could be stored over the winter months in caves, so, in a more sophisticated way, could ice during the summer. The ice well had to be sited carefully, for damp was as great a problem as warmth and good drainage was essential; they were therefore sited on south or west facing slopes. The egg-shaped ice well was dug down into the hill, lined with brick or stone and a domed cap built over it, the whole well then covered with clay and earth. A wooden grill was across the bottom with a drain to take the melt water to the outside, the drain having a double U-bend to prevent warm air penetrating the well. A cave-like passage gave access to the top of the ice well to allow the snow and crushed ice sheets from the nearby ponds to be put in between layers of straw, each layer being pounded down firmly with wooden rammers. The ice was cut out from the top when required. (It must be remembered that the ice would be used for cooling only.)

The only underground part of the Ice House is the egg-shaped bowl.

It is an indication of the severity of winters at that period that made the construction of ice houses a viable proposition, although later ice was regularly imported by sea from colder, northern climes.

What makes the ice house at Tapeley unusual is that except for the ice well, the whole construction is above ground and it shows how it works – presumably the thickness of the brickwork provided enough insulation. A somewhat similar one at Holkham Hall in Norfolk is insulated by thatch.

TAVISTOCK

The Pimple

On the eastern side of Tavistock, Down Road winds its way up 300ft to Whitchurch Down, a large open expanse of close-cropped turf, gorse bushes and a golf course over which ponies graze freely. The road was developed by the Duke of Bedford at the beginning of the twentieth century with large, detached villas, one of which was designed by Sir Edwin Lutyens. These villas needed a good water supply, so, in 1906, on the highest point of the down, an underground reservoir was constructed, covered with turf and with a little building on top to give access into it, the architect again being Lutyens!

The Pimple, as it has become known, is triangular, with 15ft walls built on a circular concrete base, each wall forming a chord within the circle. It is 8ft high with a steeply-pitched roof; on one side there is a door, while the other two have wooden slats on the exposed concrete base, where people can sit and admire the incredible view.

To the west can be seen Carridon Hill, the Cheesewring and the chimney on Craddock Moor; to the south the wooded estuary of the River Tamar and to the north and east the south-west fringes of Dartmoor – White Tor, Cox Tor, Vixen Tor, Feather Tor, and in the far distance, North Hessory Tor and its mast.

The reservoir was eventually taken over by the local water authority and in 2000, the Pimple itself was put up for sale for £1. It was bought by a local benefactor and given to the town. (Lutyens must have been fond of triangular buildings, for on the village green at Mells, Somerset, is a little open-sided, triangular shelter also designed by him.)

The 'Pimple', looking north-east towards Dartmoor. Looks can be deceptive for the building is in fact triangular.

TAWSTOCK

St Peter's Church

Unlike most village churches, St Peter's is nowhere near the centre of Tawstock, but about half a mile down a steep, winding lane between Tawstock Court, with its Elizabethan gatehouse, and the River Taw. The church has a central tower, and the different ages when it was built can be seen in the architecture and the memorials to the inhabitants of Tawstock Court. It has two unique features; one on the outside of the south porch, and the other under the tower in the crossing.

The sundial, made by John Berry of Muddiford, Somerset, in 1757, not only shows the time in Britain, but also when it is midday in Europe's capital cities and even as far away as Babylon, Madras, Boston and Samarkand! Also engraved on it are the lines of the Equator, the Tropics of Cancer and Capricorn, as well as the signs of the zodiac. It must have been of great importance to those living at Tawstock Court, but had little practical use before the days of telephonic communications!

There are four pews in the crossing, each with an elaborately carved sixteenth-century bench end, three being typical of the period, the Arms of Henry VIII, with a pomegranate, the emblem of his third wife, Catherine of Aragon, a Tree of Life incorporating the Bouchier (former owners of Tawstock Court) knot and a grotesque with monsters. It is the fourth which is so fascinating, for it represents a Hinky-Punk. These were legendary two-legged creatures who were supposed to have been the original inhabitants of Dartmoor and other wild places. The good ones guided travellers across treacherous ground, but the bad, mischievous ones would lure the unwary into bogs and wet places, then sit on their hunkers (dialect for rear quarters) on top of a tussock, laughing at the antics of their victims floundering in the mire! It is easy to see the connection with Jack-o-lanthorns and Will-o-the-Wisps, those ghostly blue flames which flickered over bogs and led travellers away from their path. (The flames were the spontaneous combustion of methane gas emitted from bogs.)

The 'Hinky-Punk'.

Called 'Spunkies' in Somerset and connected to the present day 'Punky Nights', and in the Midlands travellers would have been 'Poake-Leaden'. Shakespeare featured mischievous sprites leading characters astray: Puck in *A Midsummer Night's Dream* and also Ariel in *The Tempest*, who leads Caliban and the drunken Stephano and Trinculo up to their necks in 'the filthy mantled pool', which prompts Stephano to say to Caliban, 'Monster, your fairy, which you say is a harmless fairy, has done little better than played the Jack [Jack-o-Lanthorn] with us'.

The craftsman who carved the bench end must have had a mischievous sense of humour for perpetuating old folklore in a church setting!

118

Map Ref
SX667907

The Three Hares on a boss in St Michael's at Throwleigh and the adjoining boss which shows a Green Man. *(© The Three Hares Project, www.chrischapman photography.com)*

THROWLEIGH

The Three Hares

The hare can be found in the mythology of many religions and countries throughout the world; the hare's unusual behaviour, particularly at night, when they could often be seen 'dancing' in the fields, led them to be linked with witches and witchcraft. It was also widely believed that they were hermaphroditic and could, besides procreating without a male, give birth without losing their virginity.

It is, therefore, easy to see how the hare became associated with the Virgin Mary in the Christian religion and that three hares, linked together by one ear each to form a circle, could become a symbol of the Trinity. Small wonder, then, that the Three Hares can be found prominent on a boss in a church roof, often in close proximity to that

image of a far older belief – the Green Man – as they are in the little medieval, granite-built church of St Mary at Throwleigh.

Devonshire is particularly rich in such motifs, with seventeen churches recorded as having them, most being medieval and all being slightly different from each other, proving that they were carved by different craftsmen and at different times.

Although these churches tend to be concentrated on the eastern and north-eastern fringes of Dartmoor, they are widespread across the county – from Paignton in the south to Ashreigney in the north, from Broadclyst in the east to Kelly in the west.

There is now a 'Three Hares Project' investigating and recording these motifs throughout the country and across Europe, but no contemporary written account of their meaning has yet come to light. Although prominently placed, usually on a boss on the ceiling of the chancel or nave, they can be difficult to see in dimly-lit churches.

TIVERTON

Lady Isabella's Leat

119
Map Ref
SS975155–
SS954123

In 1250, Isabella de Fortibus, Countess of Devon, gave the town a 5½-mile long waterway, known as the Town Leat, so that it might have an adequate supply of water both for its inhabitants and their livestock. From its source below Vanpost Hill (SS975155), a small stream follows its natural course for about 2 miles, but from Norwood (SS965061) it flows in an artificial contour leat until it reaches the town, where it is conducted in a stone channel, until it at last sinks at Cogan's Well. This watercourse is still highly regarded by the town's people and every seven years, it is perambulated in a ceremony known as 'water-bailing'. The Bailiff of the Hundred is preceded by

Lady Isabella's leat in Castle Street, Tiverton.

six 'pioneers' who, with spades, axes and crowbars, ensure the channel is free from obstructions and that its banks are good. Then follow 'withy-boys' who whip the stream with withy wands, for which, in 1600, they were paid two pence each, but with inflation, had increased to a shilling in 1968! The origin of the name Cogan's Well, where the leat sinks, is not known, but it is here that the proclamations are read at the start of Tiverton's ancient charter fairs in June and October.

120

Map Ref
SS954123

TIVERTON

To a Midwife

St George's is a charming eighteenth-century church, complete with a gallery around three sides of its interior. On the front, there is a memorial to Samuel Wesley, brother of the famous John, but far more unusual is the stone memorial mounted on the outside of the south wall, which reads:

> Near this place lyeth the body of Ann Clark of this town,
> midwife, who departed this life the 12th day of January 1733.
> On harmless babes I did attend,
> While I on earth my life did spend;
> To help the helpless in their need,
> I ready was with care and speed.
> Many from pain my hands did free,
> But none from Death could rescue me.
> My glass is run and all is past,
> And yours is coming all so fast.
> John Brailey was the first child she received into the world in
> 1698 and since
> then above Five Thousand.'
> William Davey

This stone memorial was set up shortly after Ann's death by William Davey, in gratitude for her work.

Tiverton, at that time, was an extremely wealthy wool town and its prosperity and promising future must have had a profound effect on the fecundity of its population, although, sadly, many of the babies Ann Clark delivered would not have reached childhood, let alone adulthood.

121

Map Ref
SX968875

TOPSHAM

The Strand

There can be no mistaking Topsham's maritime history when visiting the town today, for it was once a thriving little port which for many centuries, rivalled Exeter in the export of woollen cloth to the Low Countries.

In the thirteenth century, the good burghers of Exeter had annoyed Isabella, Countess of Devon, so much that she punished the city by having a weir built across the River Exe (Countess Weir), so depriving

Exeter's busy port of access to the sea. It was not until the Exeter Canal was constructed in 1565 (England's first pound lock canal) so bypassing the weir, that Exeter could regain its part in exporting cloth – for, after all, Exeter was the business centre for the county's woollen industry, and it was here that the Woolen Guilds had their headquarters.

Even after Exeter once again became a competitor for trade, Topsham thrived, for it had had a head start. Many of the more affluent merchants built their houses near the strand upon which their ships could be beached for loading and unloading. Because there was more exporting than importing of goods, their vessels had often to return under ballast, usually Dutch bricks, so many houses were built solely of brick. Due to the close association the merchants and traders had with Holland, they also 'imported' the ideas of Dutch architecture.

The 'Dutch' street.

Coming from old Topsham, with its narrow, twisting streets, so redolent of the medieval port, down river to The Strand, one is suddenly transported to a Dutch street, but with the wide estuary of the River Exe on one side instead of a canal.

TORQUAY

Kent's Cavern

122
Map Ref
SX934641

Although not on the scale of other cave systems open to the public, Kent's Cavern's interest lies in the part they played in the development of scientific thought during the middle years of the nineteenth century, particularly Darwinism.

The caves are said to have been known to the Romans, but their first mention as 'Kent's Cavern' appeared in 1659. The story of the little dog which once entered them, so giving them their name, can be discounted!

> And he went and he went
> Until he coomed out
> In the county of Kent.

The caves were formed by water percolating down through the joints and fissures of the Middle and Upper Devonian Limestone and gradually enlarging them. Over thousands of years, four distinct periods occurred when the caves became dry, enabling them to be occupied by animals which are now long-extinct. Between these periods the water seeping through the limestone caused sheets of stalagmite to form on the floor, burying the bones and teeth of the former occupants and more importantly, man-made flint tools, these becoming much better made in the higher levels, thus showing that man had inhabited the land at the same periods as the animals.

This phenomena was first discovered in 1824 by John Macenvoy, the Catholic priest at Torre Abbey, who reported his findings to the British Association. They were greeted with ridicule, for had not Bishop Ussher categorically stated in his *Chronology of the Scriptures* that man did not appear on earth until 4004 BC, long after the remains of the animals found in the caves had become extinct!

However, in 1846, a local self-taught scientist, mathematician and teacher, William Pengelly, carried out further and more extensive excavations, uncovering in the various layers the bones and teeth of cave lions, sabre-toothed tigers, mammoth, woolly rhinoceros and hyenas together with more flint tools in each layer.

The results of Pengelly's investigations were reported to the British Association, the Royal Society of Antiquarians and the Royal Society in 1859. This was the year in which Charles Darwin published his *On the Origin of Species*, which made Pengelly's discoveries 'not only credible but essential' and made Darwin's work 'both credible and essential for the works of one complemented the other'. Bishop Ussher's chronology could at last be consigned to the wastebin.

Such was the high regard in which Pengelly's work was held that in 1864, the British Association granted him £2,000 to carry out further excavations in Kent's Cavern, and over the next few years, he systematically plotted the position of all the major fragments of bone, flint tool and artefact, and recorded the layer in which they were found.

Although today the caves are a major tourist attraction (especially in poor weather, for the cave's temperature remains at a constant 14°c), their historical significance is largely overlooked.

TORQUAY

123
Map Ref
SX 922666

A Model Village, Babbacombe

During the Enlightenment of the eighteenth and early nineteenth centuries, many wealthy estates built villages for their workers and tenants; however, it wasn't until the middle of the twentieth century that Babbacombe built a village – but not to be lived in, only to be looked at and admired, for it is truly a model village.

Tom Dobbins (1918–97) had always been fascinated by models, especially houses, and was determined to build the finest model village in the country. His first attempt, in 1956, was at his hometown of

Southport; however, when a superb location came onto the market on the Downs at Babbacombe, one of the country's most prestigious seaside resorts, he bought the site, moved there, and opened his model village to the public in 1963. It was quite small at first, featuring a typical Devon farmstead and an exact copy of Cockington village (an actual conservation village between Torquay and Paignton). Where this differed from other model villages (in Gloucestershire, Buckinghamshire and on the Isle of Wight) were the miniature inhabitants – Cockington even features Queen Elizabeth's visit in the 1960s.

Over the succeeding years, the 'village' has grown to include such objects as a watermill, a windmill, the Meet of a hunt outside 'Lord Elpus Hall' and even a fire engine attending a thatch fire! Like all villages, it has grown over time, with modern estates, shopping centres, representative examples of architecture from around the country and now a modern town, complete with neon signs, a railway station, a hydro-electric power station and satellite dishes. History has not been forgotten, for there is a model Stonehenge and a turf White Horse, and from an appropriate book, Gulliver being bound by the Lilliputians!

Every building and object in the village is duplicated in storerooms and workshops, so that when repairs or re-painting is required there is no disruption to the displays or for the visitors, for everything can be instantly replaced.

Set in a glorious position overlooking the sea and Babbacombe beach (not the nudist beach depicted in the village!), the model village is situated amid beautiful lawns and rare shrubs and trees. Something new is added to the model each year, making it the finest in the country and making Dobbins' dream come true. The village is open all year with free car parking.

Cockington village on the occasion of Queen Elizabeth II's visit.

124

Map Ref

SX918678

TORQUAY

Brunel Manor

The name Isambard Kingdom Brunel (1806–59) is known to everyone as England's most brilliant engineer, especially since events marking the 200th anniversary of his birth. But how many know that he had aspirations to become an owner of a large country estate and was also an enthusiastic gardener?

While developing the railways of South Devon, Brunel frequently stayed at Torquay, which by that time, had become a popular holiday resort, and during his frequent drives along the coast he would stop at the top of Watcombe Hill and admire the view to Babbacombe Downs and across the stretch of Torbay. In 1847, during one such drive, he discovered that much of the hillside, then open fields, was for sale. He thus bought the land (gradually acquiring some 500 acres over the years) on which to build his dream country house.

Although he soon had plans for his home, Brunel firmly believed that a garden should be established ten years before the house was built; so he immediately engaged Alexander Forsyth, who had just laid out the gardens at Alton Towers, as his gardener. He first planted a shelter-belt of mature trees on top of the hill to protect his grounds, developing a special machine to lift them. (Similar machines are still produced, although they are now hydraulic.) He then planted an arboretum and pinetum with such exotic trees as Chilian Pine, Sequoia and Chinese Spruce, many of which still survive. On his visits, which were often weekly, he would measure the diameters of

The view over to Babbacombe Downs and the sea (the latter is now obscured by trees).

the trees to see how they were growing in their positions. Brunel personally ensured that his huge staff of gardeners (over seventy) were well paid and well housed, and their children educated. There was, however, one serious problem – the lack of water on his estate; but, after all, he was an engineer, and about a mile away at the bottom of the hill in Moor Lane, he had five wells dug, with a steam engine to pump the water up to reservoirs.

To enable him to be on the spot whenever he could (in fact he spent more time in his garden than on any of his engineering projects), Brunel rented Watcombe Court, a large house at the bottom of the hill where he, his wife and three children lived, with a full complement of staff, for nearly nine years. His estate extended to the coast at Great Rock where he built a summer-house, with easy access to Watcombe beach. Although the cellars and foundations of the house he had planned were built, Brunel died in 1859 before it was completed, and the present house, built on the original foundations in 1870, is not to his designs.

Although the gardens at Brunel Manor now only extend to 31 acres, with some of his woodland owned by Torbay Council and open to the public, much of the former are as they were built and laid out, and there are plans for a complete restoration of the area of the grounds remaining. True to Brunel's wish that the garden be open for all to visit and enjoy, the present owners of Brunel Manor, the Christian Holiday and Conference Centre, encourage visitors to wander the grounds free of charge, but welcome contributions towards the full restoration. For further details, telephone 01803 329333.

TOTNES

The Brutus Stone

125
Map Ref
SX801604

When Geoffrey of Monmouth wrote his *History of the Kings of England* (1147), he quoted as his source 'the most ancient book in the British tongue' (of which there is no record before or since). He was also a great and imaginative spinner of tales and English literature would be poorer were it not for the myths that stemmed from his pen. With King Arthur and Merlin, he gave Malory his *Morte d'Arthur*; Shakespeare his *King Lear* and *Cymbeline*; Tennyson his *Idylls of the King* and to the city of Bath and its springs, the story of its founding by King Blabud, along with many others.

All these stories started at Totnes and with Brutus, whose great-great-grandfather was Aeneas, another weaver of tales. Brutus' mother died at his birth, and at the age of fifteen, he accidentally shot his father with an arrow while out hunting, for which he was banished

Were it not for the arrow, it might be missed!

from Italy – as it had been predicted by the gods that he would kill both his parents! After inflicting revenge upon the Greeks for the defeat at Troy, Brutus sailed away to found a new kingdom. The goddess Diana came to him in a dream and told him he would find a verdant island– Albion; after sailing up a wide, wooded river, he landed and founded the kingdom of Britain, calling its inhabitants Britons, after his name.

Halfway up the hill to the settlement, at its summit, Brutus sat down on a granite block and said, in perfect metrical English:

Here I stand, and here I rest,
And this place shall be called Totnes

After such a long sea voyage his legs probably wouldn't take him any further!

The Brutus Stone can still be seen today, beside 51 Fore Street, marked by a large arrow pointing downwards –for its top is now level with the pavement and has been polished by thousands of feet.

That is the story, and although its veracity is open to question, the townspeople think enough of the story to have the mayor, in full regalia, stand upon the stone to read the Royal Proclamation on the accession of a new sovereign.

126
Map Ref
SX800604

TOTNES

The East Gate

For 8 miles the River Dart gave easy access to the rich heartland of Devon, and Totnes provided the bulwark to prevent raiders coming any further. It had a castle on top of the prominent hill and the town was strongly walled, with four gateways. (Probably the truer origin of the name, Totnes, is from the Saxon *tot* meaning hill, and *nes* meaning nose).

The south and west gates disappeared years ago to help ease traffic congestion on market days; the north gate is in ruins and only a short length of the old town wall now stands. The east gate, however, survives and forms a prominent feature in this historic town.

The gateway stands astride the main street leading up from the river. In medieval times, it marked the eastern boundary of the town;

today it marks the meeting of Fore Street, below, and High Street above. Its archway is, fortunately, wide enough to take even modern traffic, and although the narrow passage, wide enough to take one person, has gone, there are stone steps up to the old wall. In Tudor times, the gateway was embellished with a lavishly panelled room above it, with an east-facing oriel window looking down to the river, as well as fenestrations, a clock and a belfry. In 1990 there was a disastrous fire in which the structure was badly damaged, but it has since been restored to its original beauty.

Traffic through the town now mainly follows a one-way system and can become congested in summer – but then, the best way to appreciate the town's architecture and history is on foot!

UFFCULME

The Shambles

127
Map Ref
ST067127

The Shambles in the centre of the Square at Uffculme is a rare relic from the time when purveyors of poultry, meat, dairy produce and fish would come into the town on certain days – not necessarily on a market day – to sell their goods from permanent, roofed, open-sided counters.

The one at Uffculme, dating from around the eighteenth century, was for the sale of meat only and measured 13ft by 9ft, with a steeply-pitched slate roof and carved barge boards.

It became disused when a butcher opened a shop in the town, but has now found another use; being conveniently close to a bus stop, the counter was removed and replaced by benches, making a comfortable bus shelter.

UGBOROUGH

The Sign of the Owl

About half a mile from where the B3196 leaves the A30, a narrow minor road joins from the north, with the name of the junction neatly painted down the fingerpost – 'Sign of the Owl'. Close by is a square post-medieval directional stone with a letter on each side: M (Modbury, B (Brent), T (Totnes) and K (Kingsbridge) – but nothing obviously connecting it with the name of the X-road.

In 1803, the Ordnance Survey got it almost correctly, for the 2:1 mile surveyor's map shows the junction as 'Sandoul Cross'; however, the Tithe Apportionment Map of 1842 gives the name 'Sign of the Owl' to an adjacent small arable field (later a plantation) and that name was given in about 1885 to the Ordnance Survey when making their 25in: 1 mile County Series map, as the name of the X-road. Bearing in mind how broad the Devonshire dialect was at that time, it is hardly surprising that errors and corruptions occurred.

'Sandoul' was the phonetic interpretation given in 1803 to the original Saxon word *sandauld*, meaning a tree or stone. In this context, this would have indicated that there was a 'waymark' there, showing the traveller which way to go, for the trackway coming in from the north had once been an important route, going as far back as the Bronze Age. Of course, the present stone was a much later replacement and the name of the X-road a survivor from history.

WOOLHANGER

The Music Room

129
Map Ref
SS698453

The manor of Woolhanger is first mentioned in 1282 as belonging to the Pynes, an ancient Devonian family who held it for 500 years. It was eventually inherited by a young lady, Francis Roe, who, in 1889, married nineteen-year-old Sir Henry Palk Carew, the ninth baronet of another old Devonshire family. They both loved music, especially organ music, so after setting up home at Woolbanger, they built a music room – and what a music room it was!

The Music Room in 1997, before its restoration.

It was octagonal in shape and at 55ft to the top of the rectangular lantern, glazed on all sides with stained glass, it towered over the old buildings. Two massive stone fireplaces, each bearing the Carew coat of arms, were flanked by four Gothic stone windows containing sixteen stained-glass medallion portraits depicting famous composers and writers. Opposite the main doorway leading into the room was a full-sized church organ, made by a leading maker, Vowles of Bristol. The organ needed far more air than could be provided by hand so a large bellows was installed, driven, via gearing, chain drive and lay-shafting, by a water-wheel over 90ft away. The water for this was provided by a pond constructed high on the moor half a mile away, through a 9in cast-iron pipe.

The music room was acoustically perfect and was, in fact, a small concert hall. The couple both played

well, but on special occasions, a coach would fetch Dr Edwards, an accomplished organist, from Barnstaple.

No account has survived of any grand musical event, and when, after fifteen years, the Carews left, the succeeding owners had no use for a music room and it fell gradually into decay. The organ was sold to a large church in the north of England; the water-wheel for a time worked at a small sawmill; the medallion-portraits were sent to Christies and sold to America, and the oak flooring finished up as pigsties. The shell finally became a furniture repository for Pickfords to hold furniture from bombed houses in Plymouth and Exeter. A sad end for this grand Victorian Gothic building – except that it was not the end.

The property was recently acquired by Mr G.F.C. Mellstrom, who had already bought the Woolhanger farms. The old farmhouse has been completely renovated and turned into an extremely comfortable country house, with views over the lake and Chapman Barrows on Exmoor. The music room is currently being restored to its original grand design, which even English Heritage could not better! It is doubtful, though, if there will ever be a full-size organ again and the medallion-portraits are irreplaceable, but the lantern will once again glow with light and the Gothic splendour of the interior restored to its former glory. A happy ending, which only a decade ago would have seemed impossible.

YARCOMBE

130

Map Ref
51234060

Fort Cottage

Near the parish boundary between Yarcombe and Stockland, at the very top of Rower Hill (689ft), are the remains of Fort Cottage. This once thatched cottage was only small – two up and two down – but the crenulated front was built high and square with a small viewing tower in the centre and an oval plaque 'OLD 1821'.

It was built by the son of Major General Elliot Drake (yes, the same famous family) of Sheafhayne Manor, on the southernmost edge of his Yarcombe estate, for one of his gamekeepers. (Presumably the viewing tower was used as a lookout for poachers.) During the early years of the last century it was occupied by the Doble family, which consisted of eleven children, and later during the Second World War, by two elderly ladies. There was no electricity and no piped water, only an 80ft well with a bucket, and windless. Their cottage had not even a path leading up to it across the fields, let alone a track! It was aptly named, for the high crenulations of the little house stood out

Fort Cottage
before conversion,
c. 1985.

starkly against the sky on its lofty eminence. It has now been rebuilt,
and much enlarged as a country residence with more crenulations
than the original.

131
Map Ref
SX579517

YEALMPTON

Old Mother Hubbard

When Sarah Catherine Martin was a young woman she was a frequent visitor to Kitley Park near Yelverton, the home of her brother-in-law, John Bastard MP. She was a chatterbox and one day John, wanting a little peace to write his letters, asked her 'to run away and write one of your stupid little rhymes'. The result was one of the best known nursery rhymes, 'The Comic Adventures of Old Mother Hubbard and Her Dog', consisting of fourteen verses, the first being:

> Old Mother Hubbard
> Went to the cupboard
> To get her poor dog a bone,
> When she got there
> The cupboard was bare
> So the poor dog had none.

Old Mother
Hubbard's
Cottage, c. 1930.
(William Davies)

Sarah's rhyme was published and within a year, her illustrated version had sold 10,000 copies. The real Mother Hubbard was thought to have been a housekeeper to the Bastard family, and on retirement she was given the cottage to live in.

Sarah was an attractive young woman and when she was seventeen years old, she fell in love with Prince William Henry, the future King William IV, while he was visiting Kitley. The love was reciprocated, but because of their different stations in life, could come to nought.

The cupboard in the cottage is now far from bare, for it has become a pleasant little restaurant serving good food and wine.

BIBLIOGRAPHY & SOURCES

'Babbacombe Model Village – A Guide', 2007

Baring-Gould, S., *Devonshire Characters and Strange Events*, Bodley Head, 1926

Baring-Gould, S., *Devon*, Anthony Mott, 1983, f/p 1899

Beaumont, G.F., *The Story of Combe Martin*, privately published, 2000

Bickley, F., *Where Dorset Meets Devon*, Constable, 1911

Blackmore, R.D., *Perlycross*, 1894

Blackmore, R.D., *Lorna Doone*, 1869

Burton, S.H., *A West Country Anthology*, Robert Hale, 1975

Cambell, D., *Exploring the Undercliff*, Coastal Publishing, Wareham, 2006

Chard, J., *Devon Mysteries*, Bossiney Books, Bodmin, 1979

Cherry, B. & Pevsner, N., *Buildings of England, Devon*, Penguin, 1989

Church Notes: St Blaize, Haccombe, St Mary, Ottery St Mary; St Peter, Tawstock

Clinton-Badderly, V.G., *Devon*, A. & C. Black, 1925

Cooksey, A.J.A., *Admiralty Signals & Telegraph Stations*

Coulter, J., *The Hinky-Punk*, Tawstock Parochial Church Council, 2001

Crossing, W., *Guide to Dartmoor*, David & Charles, Newton Abbot, 1965

County Guides, *Devon*, Penguin, 1939

Dartmoor National Park, HMSO Guide, 1957

Devon C.C., *Devon's Heritage Buildings and Landscape*, Devon County Council, 1982

Ewans, M.C., *The Haytor Granite Railway & Stover Canal*, David & Charles, Newton Abbot, 1964

Fielder, D., *A History of Bideford*, Phillimore, Chichester, 1985

Freeman, R., *Remember D-Day*, Dartmouth History Research Group, 1994

Fuller, I., Revd, *Worthies of England*, 1664

Gerrish, T., *Devon off the Beaten Track*, Countryside Books, Newbury, 2002

Griffiths, G.D. & E.G.C., *History of Teignmouth*, Brunswick Press, Teignmouth, 1973

Grigson, G., *West Country*, Collins, 1951

Gunnell, C., *My Dartmoor*, Bossiney Books, Bodmin, 1977

Hadfield, C., *Canals of South West England*, David & Charles, Newton Abbot, 1987

Hannigan, D., *Eccentric Britain*, New Holland, 2004

Harvey, U.L., *The Tragedy of Hallsands Village*, privately published

Headley, G., & Meulenkemp, W., *Follies*, Jonathan Cape, 1989

Heath, S., *The South Devon & Dorset Coast*, T. Fisher Unwin, 1910

Holmes, R., *Hottentot Venus: The Life & Death of Saartjie Baartman*, Bloomsbury, 2007

Hoskin, W.G., *Old Devon*, Pan, 1966

Illustrated History of Dartmoor, Ward Lock, 1889

Jenkins, S., *England's Thousand Best Churches*, Penguin, 2000

Kelly, A., *Mrs Coade's Stone*, Self Publishing Association, 1990

Knowling, P., *Dartmoor Follies*, Orchard Publishing, Devon, 2002

Lambton, L., *Magnificent Menagerie*, Harper Collins, 1992

Lyson, D. Revd, & Lyson, S., *Magna Britannia*, Devon, 1822

Madge, R., *Railways Round Exmoor*, Exmoor Press, Dulverton, 1975

Mee, A., *The King's England: Devon*, Hodder & Stoughton, 1965

Norway A.H., *Highways & Byways in Devon & Cornwall*, Macmillan, 1911

Owen, A.N., *History of a Devon Custom*, self published, 2006

Polwhele, R. Revd, *History of Devonshire*, 1796

Ponsford, C.N., *Time in Exeter*, Headwell Vale Books, Exeter, 1995

Risdon, T., *Chorographical Description & Survey of Devon*, 1811

Russell, P., *History of Torquay*, Torquay Natural History Society, 1960

Salmon, A.L., *Dartmoor*, Blackie, 1920

Shore, H.N., Com., The Hon., R.N., *Smuggling Days & Smuggling Ways*, Cassell, 1892

Softly, B., *Tapping at the Garden Gate*, Westcountry Books, 1995

St Leger-Gordon, D., *Devonshire*, Robert Hale, 1955

St Leger-Gordon, R., *The Witchcraft and Folklore of Dartmoor*, Robert Hale, 1965

Timpson, J., *Timpson's England*, Jarrold, 1987

Warren, D., *East Devon Curiosities*, Obelisk Press, Exeter, 1999

Webber, R., *The Devon & Somerset Blackdown Hills*, Robert Hale, 1976

Wickings, J., *Norman Lockyer & His Observations*, Sidmouth Astronomical Society, 2003

Willy, M., *The South Hams*, Robert Hale, 1955

Wreford, H. & Williams, M., *Mysteries in the Devon Landscape*, Bossiney Books, St Teath, 1985